CULTURE LEARNING

The Art of Understanding What No One Can Teach You

MARK HEDINGER

EDITED BY RACHEL ASKEW

CULTURE LEARNING
The Art of Understanding What No One Can Teach You

Self-published by Mark Hedinger
Shared through the ministry of CultureBound
PO Box 16716
Portland, OR 97292 USA

All rights reserved. No part of this book may be reproduced or used in any form without written permission from the author.

The websites and resources recommended in this book are intended to be helpful for further study. The use of these sites does not imply an endorsement for this book, nor do we vouch for their content.

Unless otherwise noted, all Scripture quotations are taken from THE HOLY BIBLE English Standard Version. Biblica, 2011. Bible Gateway, https://www.biblegateway.com/versions/English-Standard-Version-ESV-Bible/

© 2021, Mark Hedinger
Published by CultureBound

ISBN 979-8-9853721-3-7

The CultureBound Team: Karen Hedinger, Terry Steele, Rachel Askew, Jon Mazarella, Kylie Trout, Jacob Huey, Natalie Kim
Cover Design: Rachel Askew

Lovingly dedicated to Karen, my lifetime partner in culture learning.

Contents

Acknowledgements	9
1. The Journey	11
2. Every Nation	16
3. Envisioning the Invisible	24
4. Relationship Patterns	35
5. Learning About Culture	47
6. The Mental Model	57
7. The Languages of Culture	77
8. Active Learning Skills	92
9. Active Learning Attitudes	108
10. Tying it All Together	129
Endnotes	135
Author Information	139
Notes Pages	141

Acknowledgements

This work has been a labor of love for the staff and friends of a ministry called CultureBound, with offices in Portland, Oregon, United States. This book is truly the result of a group project and represents the most exciting collaboration in my many years of Christian ministry. From a variety of generations, nationalities, and experiences, we have journeyed with each other in the fullness that this book describes.

This book is also built on the foundations of others who came before us. I am grateful for the missiologists, communicologists, anthropologists, and sociologists of many nations who have contributed ideas to help those journeying across cultures. Those ideas are foundational for us, and you will see references to many authors and researchers as you work through the book. I am also thankful for the students who listened, interacted, and helped to shape the ideas of this book – some from CultureBound courses and others from formal programs at Western Seminary in Portland, Oregon.

Thanks to Dr. Donald K. Smith, the founder of the organization that has come to be known as CultureBound. His insights on communicating across cultural landscapes are foundational to culture learning, and to my life and service in Christian ministry.

Thanks to Dr. Enoch Wan of Western Seminary whose relational transformation paradigm is foundational to this book. From a biblical and practical point of view, learning to live and work in healthy vertical and horizontal relationships is central to culture learning.

I am blessed beyond measure to work with the CultureBound team, past and present. These friends and coworkers have shaped the ideas in this book. They all have contributed to the practice and concepts of culture learning for the sake of gospel transformation that extends into unfamiliar cultures and languages.

With deep gratitude I would like to thank the CultureBound team, listed here in alphabetical order: Rachel Askew, Karen Hedinger, Jacob Huey, Natalie Kim, Jon Mazarella, Terry Steele, Kylie Trout, Mark Vance, and Lauren Wells.

For team CultureBound, past and present, and for those authors and scholars whose work shaped this – thank you.

CHAPTER ONE

The Journey

This is a book about a journey, but it's not really about a change of location. The journey you will learn about takes place within. The goal is to transform your mind and heart so that you can connect with the mind and heart of another human being who sees life much differently than you.

Journeys can be powerful, even epic at times! Think about the journey of an American couple, packing up their household and moving with young children to live and work in Mexico. They initially thought the change of location would be the most significant adjustment. What they learned over time was that the changes to their life patterns were even more powerful. The journey of their hearts and minds included everything from new ways of eating to new habits of understanding human relationships. The journey of changing their patterns of life, it turns out, was much more significant than the change of location.

Some physical journeys can be short and appear insignificant. You can walk to the grocery store or the neighborhood gym without much of that "epic" feeling. As you make that short walk, however, you pass the homes of migrants, refugees, and newcomers from all over the world right in your own neighborhood. They are on much of the same journey as the couple in Mexico. They are learning to live and work where the patterns of thought, relationship, daily life, and cycles of life are very different than what they grew up with! The journey they are taking is so much more difficult and profound than the voyage that brought them here.

The important, significant journey comes from growth in your heart and mind. As you discover this deeper journey into understanding, you will find that learning a series of cultural "rules" is not enough.

The goal is to transform your mind and heart so that you can connect with the mind and heart of another human being who sees life much differently than you.

Sure, you can read all the books that try to explain a specific culture, but none of them are anywhere near adequate. Sometimes, those books make sweeping generalizations that are misleading. There is always a range of personality within any group of people. Some people will react and respond in ways that are not within their traditional cultural patterns.

Other times, books that attempt to describe cultures are not able to adequately talk about regional, generational, or economic differences. Those attempts at describing people in generic terms actually get in the way of your journey to the hearts and minds of your neighbors.

Maybe you have been wanting to make a physical journey or wanting to welcome refugees into your community. In either case, this book will not give you generalizations about cultures. This book will give you tools to be self-directed in learning the perspectives of those around you. This book will help to bridge the gap from your heart to theirs, from your way of thinking to theirs, from your way of shaping relationships to theirs. This book is the self-directed learner's guide to cross-cultural relationships. As it says in the subtitle, this book is about the art of understanding what no one can teach you.

This book is written from a Christian point of view. You will notice biblical references throughout. You will notice the expectation of involvement from the Father, Son, and Holy Spirit as you make the journey across cultures.

It is assumed that most readers will be part of a local gathering of believers, like a church or congregation. That is not a requirement, but you will notice this underlying assumption throughout.

This is also written to people who have some understanding of mission work, both in biblical contexts and practical outreach in the 21st century. If you don't have that background, don't worry! You will still benefit from the stories and concepts that grow from Christian mission.

Finally, this is written to all who are on that journey from one way of life and ministry to another. Perhaps your passport says you come from Argentina, or perhaps from the United States – that doesn't matter. If you are involved with ministry across cultures, this book is meant for you.

The approaches in this book include ideas that have not always been common for cross-cultural training. The following points are foundational to the CultureBound approach.

- This is a guide for self-directed learning rather than a summary of all the anthropology or communication science that is typically taught in cross-cultural training.
- Relationships are the focus of this book. Other approaches focus on cultural trends in general terms. This book will help map the journey from one human to another in relational terms.

- The approach written here is a journey of mind and heart, with insights from the world of neurobiology and awareness of attitudes.
- This approach begins with an understanding that culture is the study of life patterns for any group of people. These patterns form a cohesive, holistic way of life.

A NOTE FROM THE AUTHOR

Culture learning is a beginning, not an end. I have tried to describe the journey that will lead to healthy relationships across cultures. I have included some stories and shared some principles. I have tried to explain the journey of being self-directed at learning an unfamiliar culture.

I realize the risk that this written volume can pose. There are highs, lows, variations, and different perceptions in culture learning. I believe that most readers will benefit greatly from working through this book as part of a guided cohort, sharing with each other under the guidance of an experienced facilitator.

 **This book is the self-directed learner's guide to cross-cultural relationships.**

I would humbly ask that you see this book as one leg of a chair. If you try to sit on a chair with only one leg, it will at best be uncomfortable and at worst lead to injury! The chair is much more solid, comfortable, and trustworthy when it has four legs. *In the same way, this book is more beneficial when read in conjunction with a trainer, a cohort, and a guided presentation.* If you do not have a group available, consider joining a CultureBound course by visiting our website at www.CultureBound.org.

My prayer and hope is that culture learning will give you excitement, assurance, and guidance as you make your journey! May you cross the distance in your own mind and heart as a self-directed learner and enter into healthy relationships with people of other cultures.

CHAPTER TWO

Every Nation

There are over 7 billion people in the world.

Let that sink in. Your close circle of friends and family might be between 10 and 50 people. Your acquaintances might extend to a couple hundred. When you start to do the math, 7 billion becomes very difficult to comprehend.

These 7 billion people constitute over 190 countries[1], over 7,000 languages[2], and over 4,000 religions.[3]

These numbers might be overwhelming to you, but not to God. God has promised that he will be with his children as he sends them to reach every person.

Jesus made a promise that he would build his church, and that no power on earth or in heaven would stop him (Matt. 16:18). It is Jesus himself, God in the flesh, who is making that promise. He walked on water. He healed the sick and performed many miracles. He even rose from the dead! You might sometimes take for granted the idea that the son of God can accomplish a task so huge.

There's more information included in the promise to build his church. According to Revelation 5, his church will include those "from every tribe and language and people and nation (Rev. 5:9)." Let that settle in your mind.

Every tribe.
Every language.
Every people group.
Every nation.

That is a very wide, broad, and inclusive promise! You may not see how he will do it, but you can believe. It is Jesus who is building this enormous church that will have people from literally all nations and languages and cultures and customs. If he says he will bring every group together, then you can believe him. He is Jesus!

> And they sang a new song saying, 'Worthy are you to take the scroll and to open its seals, for you were slain, and by your blood you ransomed people for God from every tribe and language and people and nation...'
> Revelation 5:9

You may not have a problem believing that Jesus will keep his promises; however, you may run into some other difficulties with this "every tribe, language, people, and nation" picture.

It may be harder to process that Jesus wants to use you to accomplish his mission! He wants to use his children in the process of building his church.

That amazing promise in Matthew 16:18 is sandwiched between comments made to Simon Peter. Simon Peter will assist Jesus in his ministry. He won't just be a member, but an integral part of building the church.

John's vision of the thousands upon thousands comes just after the letters of Revelation chapters 2 and 3, addressed to local churches with human pastors and members.

There are many other passages that speak to the fact that God is using people to carry his message. Acts 1:8 calls on believers to "be my witnesses in Jerusalem and in all Judea and Samaria, and to the ends of the earth." Matthew 28:18-20 calls Jesus' followers to "make disciples of all nations."

The idea of Jesus building his church is not hard to accept. The fact that he wants to use you to build that church and take his message to the ends of the earth – that might be difficult to grasp!

What will it take to be God's witnesses to the ends of the earth? What will it take for the church to reach every tribe, language, people, and nation? How is that done now? How will it be done? If you are part of unfolding that plan, what are you supposed to do?

There are two main ways to answer those questions. You can go to the nations or you can receive people who move from the nations into your homeland.

Fulfilling that Matthew 28 command to go and make disciples means interacting with people from other tribes and tongues through short-term or long-term relationships. Through going or receiving, you can get involved in the lives of people whose language and customs are different from yours. Practically, this can include many different things. You make and eat their food. Your kids play with their kids. You cry at their funerals and invite them to cry at yours. You rejoice in their weddings and child dedications, whatever those might look like!

The call to make disciples is a call to be involved in the lives of every "tribe, language, people, and nation." The door is then open to tell them what Christ has done for you. You can teach them to know, love, and obey God. Whether you go to the nations or receive the nations into your homeland, choose to be involved with people from another culture for the sake of the gospel. As you share with the people in your circles, you can be confident that God will simultaneously have other believers involved with different tribes, languages, people, and nations.

When you seek to reach the nations, it is natural to question exactly what will successfully build relationships with those in a different culture. If you are part of the group that is carrying God's message to every tribe, language, people, and nation, what do you need to know in order to do that? Who will teach you how?

This is where there is some great news that sounds very discouraging at first. The truth is that no one can teach you how to interact with other cultures. There is no way that a book, video series, class, or teacher can tell you how to successfully integrate your life into a specific culture. No curriculum will be sufficient in explaining the cultural patterns of someone from another country who moves into your hometown. For many reasons, no one can teach you how to live in another culture.

First, it is an impossible task. Human beings interact through countless mediums – touching, preparing foods, speaking, and singing, to name a few. Clothing carries messages, color choices can be nuanced or blunt in their significance, and body language is a lifelong course on its own. There are simply too many ways that people interact. There is no way to capture a culture in an all-encompassing teaching tool.

Further, even if you could write down all the habits of heart, mind, body, and relationship that direct the life interactions of a group of people, many of those things would change again in short order. Cultures are alive. They shift and change at some levels, and stay stable across centuries at other levels. Even the most painstaking study of a culture is limited by time. Any description needs to be contextualized and will not be able to fully account for the changes of the culture before or after that time frame.

Additionally, culture cannot be understood at a purely cognitive level. Even if you had a great description of another group of people and how they live, simply "knowing" those things is not nearly the same as experiencing it, living it, sharing it, and learning it from the inside out. Real culture learning takes place less at a cognitive, thinking level and more at a far deeper, intuitive level.

If no one can teach you how to specifically live, work, and interact in an unfamiliar culture, how can you ever obey God's call to be involved with the nations around you? The discouraging news is that no one can teach you. The good news is that you can still learn.

Learning how to learn a culture is exactly the purpose for this book. You won't read about specific cultures that are found all over the earth. You will discover how to learn those cultures on your own.

The truth is no one can teach you about life in your little village of Romania or your city in South Korea. You can, however, learn the tools that will equip you to live successfully among the locals.

You can learn a culture on your own. What you need is...

...the right attitudes – how can you adjust your mindset?

...the right skills – how can you learn and how should you act in a new situation?

...the right concepts – how can you understand?

It is not hard to illustrate the importance of the idea that culture has to be learned through practice rather than theory. A young couple from the United States that arrives in Latin America has probably been told that time frames are not as strict as in the United States. The couple absorbs this information and routinely shows up late to their own appointments. One day, a friend from their new nation asks them why they are frequently late. After they explain, she says, "I know that among my people there is a reputation of not arriving on time for meetings; however, I am a very punctual person." While some generalizations are true for different cultures, there are always exceptions best learned through experience.

Think about another couple, also from the United States. When they arrived in India they were met with a wonderful, hospitable lunch reception. The cuisine was all Indian until the very end. Someone had heard that Americans like sweets. As a beautiful gesture, they brought a small dessert to the couple. While it was very thoughtful, the couple felt incredibly awkward eating the dessert by themselves. The generalities that were supposed to lead to better interaction across cultures actually caused an awkward moment.

 **The discouraging news is that no one can teach you. The good news is that you can still learn.**

These are small examples that highlight the importance of learning through experience. Books and seminars by nature present broad generalizations. Real life healthy relationships grow over time and take all kinds of unexpected twists and turns! Gaining the mindset and tools to learn on your own, in each new circumstance, will help avoid those generalities and build healthy interactions between people of different cultures.

This book is built on four ideas.
1. Jesus is building his church and it will include every tribe, language, people, and nation - literally!
2. Jesus uses people, including you, to do that work.
3. You can learn how to work and live in a culture and language different from your own.
4. Learning to work and live in an unfamiliar culture is a matter of developing healthy attitudes, skills, and concepts.

In each of the chapters that follow, you will learn about those tools. You will discover biblical illustrations, real life examples, application questions, and other practical resources. Above all, this book is built on the premise that every tribe, language, people, and nation will be around that great throne giving Jesus the worship he deserves. How will those people get there?

Those throngs of people will be around the throne of the King of Kings because someone like you was a witness to the power of God and entered their world to tell them about him. Why learn the attitudes, skills, and concepts that will help you adjust to life in another culture? You learn because you have the high calling of bringing the gospel into new homes, neighborhoods, cities, and nations. They will one day be part of every tribe, language, people, and nation.

CHAPTER REVIEW

- What does it mean to say, "No one can teach you a culture, but you can learn?"
- Why is it impossible to teach someone a culture?
- Why is it important to learn a culture?

PUT IT INTO PRACTICE

- Read Revelation 5:9 and 7:9. Can you imagine what that throng of people will be like? Can you picture every tribe, language, people, and nation all together? Let your mind and heart reflect on that beauty for a while.
- In five minutes write down all the tribes, languages, people and/or nations you can think of. How many did you come up with? If you think across history and around the globe, how many people groups could this include?

CHAPTER THREE

Envisioning the Invisible

There was a great guitar teacher named Sam. He was giving lessons to Bobby, trying with great patience and skill to help him focus on the timing and rhythms of popular folk songs. Week after week, he would model the timing that fit a given song. Bobby would try to remember and perform the exact up/down patterns that Sam had played, but it always sounded off. Both Sam and Bobby were disappointed and challenged. What wasn't Bobby hearing?

One week, Sam didn't give Bobby a pattern to follow. He turned on a recorded version of the song they were working on and asked Bobby to pay special attention to the percussion. "Listen to the drums because they will guide you to the right way to strum this song." That sounds a little odd – learn guitar by listening to the drums? The fact is, though, that it worked!

Music, like almost all of life, is not learned directly. It is learned by paying attention to the invisible. A teacher might say that her job is to "make the implicit explicit." She takes the invisible and makes it visible. She digs below the surface. She looks at the heart. There are many different metaphors that all point to the same purpose. If you want to master guitar, listen to the invisible beat that comes from the drummer. If you want to master culture, learn to see the invisible influences that work in any environment. There are five invisible influences that will guide your thinking and work in an unfamiliar culture.

INVISIBLE INFLUENCES

- Jesus
- People
- The Spirit
- Patterns
- Synchronization

INVISIBLE INFLUENCE #1: JESUS

The primary invisible factor is Jesus building his church and using people in the process. The idea of ministry with and among an unfamiliar group of people is never just a matter of human understanding. Proverbs 3 is a great focus for this concept. "Trust in the Lord with all your heart and do not lean on your own understanding. In all your ways acknowledge him and he will make straight your paths (Prov. 3:5-6)."

There is an invisible problem at the root of human involvement in ministry. Often people think that ministry is all about them simply because it involves them! The truth is that you are not equipped to design effective ministry all alone. Humans do not have the innate insight or wisdom to know who to go to – God's guidance is needed. Your direct actions don't accomplish what you want to accomplish, and there is a reason for that. Being active does not mean being in control. People are active, but only under the direction of God. Jesus is building his church through his children – they do not independently decide the steps to take.

It is important to keep this invisible influence in mind when working in ministry. Your activity in God's harvest does not imply that you are the one making decisions. You are a servant actively working under the direction and guidance of one whose understanding is so much deeper than yours. He calls you to work, but he also promises to never leave you nor forsake you. He promises to give wisdom to those who seek it. He promises to build his church!

INVISIBLE INFLUENCE #2: PEOPLE

The second invisible influence deals with the human side of ministry. Jesus gives gifts to his people, and each person has a role in his mission. If God's plan is every tribe, language, people, and nation gathered safely in his eternal presence worshiping and enjoying him forever, you might think you should drop all other activities in order to focus on reaching the unreached people.

If it were a completely human venture, maybe that would make sense. God, however, calls and equips those whom he wants to send into that multicultural work. The Bible talks of spiritual gifts. 1 Corinthians 12 is one key passage. God equips people for the different tasks that are required when ministering in an unfamiliar culture.

> Trust in the Lord with all your heart, and do not lean on your own understanding. In all your ways acknowledge him, and he will make straight your paths.
> Proverbs 3:5-6

It is God who allows you to understand the invisible motivations, beliefs, and values of a people group. It is God who allows you to adjust to other languages or cultures. God is at work bringing about the results he has in mind and equipping the ones he sends. "For it is God who works in you..." is the way Paul describes this idea in Philippians 2:13.

This is great news for those who are gifted in intercultural ministry...and even for those who are not! For those who are called to the nations, it is encouraging to know that your ability to connect with others is not something that you imagine. God really is at work, and you can enjoy his presence and guidance while serving in intercultural situations.

For those who are gifted in other areas, this means that there is no guilt for not going. There are too many people whose motivation for mission is solely the needs of people. They hear of groups who have not yet received the good news of the gospel. It touches their hearts and they want to see the best for them throughout eternity. The needs of receiving cultures are a strong motivation. The visible perspective will focus on needs.

If your eyes are solely on the needs, however, then you miss the invisible influence that calls you to look at the giver of gifts. Needs are always there. The question is, "Who has been specially equipped to serve this need?" Learning to discern the direction and gifts that God has given his people are the foundation of this second invisible influence.

INVISIBLE INFLUENCE #3: THE SPIRIT

The third invisible influence is the guidance of the Spirit. Look at the story in Acts 16 that is known as "the Macedonian call." Paul was teaching among the people of Asia when he had a distinct call to cross the Aegean Sea into what is now Greece. The Spirit called Paul to ministry and then equipped him with gifts that would allow him to be fruitful in his work. Then, the Spirit directed him to new lands.

The invisible influence that calls you and equips you with gifts for a fruitful ministry is the third person of the triune God. He calls, he provides, and he directs.

A serious concern in Christian ministry among any audience is forgetting that God is at work invisibly in those he calls AND in those he directs you to. This topic is discussed more in-depth in the next chapter through a mission principle called "the relational paradigm."

INVISIBLE INFLUENCE #4: PATTERNS

The premise of this book is that no one can teach you how to develop effective ministry in an unfamiliar culture, but that you can teach yourself with the right mix of attitudes, skills, and concepts. This is much more feasible when you consider that culture is all about patterns. Just as a given person has habits of behavior, cultures also have habits. These are a series of actions, thought patterns, beliefs, and attitudes that are normal and acceptable to those who live in that culture.

When you start looking at culture as patterns that are appropriate and acceptable to a group of people, you will quickly realize that learning a culture is all about learning their patterns of life. You come from your own people. You have patterns of life that guide you day to day. These patterns include everything from the time you get up and go to work to the deep values that resonate with you and your people. When you are among the people you grew up with, you will intuitively know the patterns of life, conversation, belief, action, calendar, and more.

Now, however, you've been sent to another group of people. They do not share your patterns. They have their own patterns of life, conversation, belief, action, and calendar. You have identified major differences between your patterns and theirs. What does this mean in terms of Christian ministry across cultures?

It means that you have to learn to build bridges. You need to learn to cross from "my patterns" to "the patterns of this unfamiliar culture." It requires a willingness to adjust your habits to this unfamiliar culture, instead of expecting them to conform to you.

INVISIBLE INFLUENCE #5: SYNCHRONIZATION

When talking about building bridges, the idea is to learn the patterns of another group of people and then synchronize your own habits with their patterns. You have a message that you want to share, but you know that interacting too directly will not be effective. Remember how important it is for guitarists to listen to the drums? A big part of your impact will come as you learn to sync your way of life, your thought patterns, your communication patterns, your teaching styles, and your values with the people you are working among.

Syncing is a beautiful dance of brain waves that goes far beyond simply pronouncing some unfamiliar sounds while learning a new language. Syncing is used to describe what occurs when two or more people are thinking in unison. Literally, their brain waves start to synchronize.[4]

The mission is to communicate God's word to people who don't know it. That communication is hindered by different patterns of life, thought, and values. The gifted intercultural worker will learn how to build a bridge that crosses from their own culture into the world of those they are sent to. Ministry is about creating understanding through mutual involvement.[5] It is about learning to sync with people from a very different set of beliefs, habits, customs, experiences, and language.

For those who are leaving their homeland to move into a culture that is unfamiliar, syncing will involve adjusting and adapting to new ways of life. Adjustment means internal, emotional modification without undue emotional stress. Adaptation refers to making lifestyle changes so that you can better live among the new people.

Think about a situation that is really quite common. A Christian who has been called and gifted for intercultural ministry moves to a land where the last meal of the day is prepared around 10:00 at night and normal bedtime is around midnight. This disciple comes from a part of the world where "early to bed, early to rise" is a virtue. What does it look like to adjust and adapt?

In this scenario, if the gospel worker wants to sync with his new neighbors, he will probably need to change both internal attitudes and external behaviors. It is likely that those meals would be a wonderful time to get to know his neighbors and talk about life. The gospel worker will want to be available, look for ways to accept invitations, and make his own invitations!

 Syncing is a beautiful dance of brain waves that goes far beyond simply pronouncing some unfamiliar sounds while learning a new language.

It is important to create open doors for the gospel, and follow Paul's model in 1 Corinthians 9.

"To the weak I became weak, that I might win the weak. I have become all things to all people, that by all means I might save some (1 Cor. 9:22)."

The early riser will need to nurture an attitude that different is not wrong. A positive feeling toward late night dinners should replace the desire to follow cultural patterns of the homeland. The virtue of going to bed early should be replaced with the virtue of forming a relationship with those who need the gospel. In order to sync, the ministry worker will need to adjust their attitudes.

The gospel worker needs more than just attitudes, though. He also needs to adjust his sleep patterns to fit the environment where he is now living. Learning how to stay up late means learning how to sleep later in the morning. It could also include learning how to take an afternoon rest time. In many parts of the world this is exactly the pattern of the people.

As the disciple learns to sync his sleep patterns to fit those of his neighbors, opportunities arise for conversations with those neighbors. Every step of being in sync will allow the gospel worker to be more involved and eventually share the gospel. Jesus' incarnational ministry put him in sync with humanity. He knows all that humanity will ever experience. He transformed his patterns, and did so without sin (Heb. 4:14–16).

The concept of synchronization is not only important for those who move into unfamiliar cultures. It is also relevant for those who want to receive people from other countries. Syncing with newcomers could look like helping them to live well in their new neighborhood. It might include deliberately creating a church culture that is flexible in service times or expressions of worship.

There is one very important clarification to add at this point. Simply adjusting or adapting to the life, thoughts, and feelings of another group of people is not a guarantee that the gospel you are sharing will be accepted. The idea of syncing opens the door for deeper conversations and gospel proclamation, but the response from people is a very different matter. The invisible influence of synchronization opens the door for clear delivery of the gospel, but it is the Word and Spirit of God that moves a person to respond to the gospel (Acts 16:14).

If you work towards synchronization, you have a tool for growth in any situation. Whether moving to a different place or welcoming new people to your home, syncing allows you to open the door and share the gospel.

INVISIBLE BUT POWERFUL

If someone tried to teach you how to interact in a new culture, they might give you direct pronouncements about what you need to do in all kinds of circumstances. It is likely that you won't remember all of those. Even if you do, you will not have a deep and heartfelt perspective on why they are important. You will act out of rote memory.

> Ministry is about creating understanding through mutual involvement.

If you keep the invisible influences in mind, then you will see a much more organic growth as you watch for God to direct, consider your own gifts, expect the Spirit to lead those who can best serve him in each context, adjust your life patterns, and make it a goal to sync with your new neighbors at home or abroad. In days gone by, the focus would've been working toward language fluency. Cultural adjustment and adaptability scales talk about learning new habits of thought or action. It will help to push the reasoning a little deeper.

Fluency or cultural adaptation are not issues in and of themselves. They are not things that one can simply learn by direct work. These are things that grow from invisible influences. If the goal is to develop a bridge – to sync – with others, then one is able to continually push to develop communication and adjust or adapt to a given situation. The motivation is completely different between trying to memorize and accomplish "the right thing," and walking in relationship with neighbors, syncing more each step of the way.

Consider this personal story of synchronization. When I lived in Mexico, I had a friend I'll call Solomon. He taught me how to live and work in his country, to the point where I was invited to be part of a leadership team with him. When leading, we would frequently reach the same conclusions at the same time. We didn't have the word "sync" in our vocabulary at the time, but the idea became clear during our interactions. Our minds learned to walk together, even though we were from two extremely different places. This synchronization was clearly a blessing from God.

The invisible influences allow you to change your attitude from "mine" and "yours" into an understanding of "ours."

CHAPTER REVIEW

- What are the five invisible influences?
- Why are each of them important to remember as you minister interculturally?
- What are some examples of synchronization that you have heard of or experienced?

PUT IT INTO PRACTICE

- Can you think of any times when you really understood an idea or a situation after you realized an invisible element of that idea? Can you talk about how the invisible helps to explain the visible?
- What are your spiritual gifts? Are you using them? Isn't it beautiful when you are serving in your strengths instead of trying to fulfill a task that you are not spiritually equipped for?
- What are some areas of church that are best served by people gifted in intercultural work?
- Have you moved or do you envision moving to another part of the world? What are some lifestyle habits that require flexibility for synchronization? What would happen if you stayed aloof in those areas? What advantages will you have if you lean into those areas and learn to adjust and adapt to a new way of life?

CHAPTER FOUR

Relationship Patterns

Now that you know and consider the invisible influences and syncing with your new neighbors, you can consider the importance of relationships. This chapter focuses on the dynamic between syncing and relationships. They are interconnected and both essential for effective work in an unfamiliar culture and language.

A BIBLICAL PERSPECTIVE

You have read about two ways to approach intercultural ministry. The first way is to memorize and cognitively grasp the patterns of a group of people with the intention of trying to recall and apply those patterns later.

The other approach is to learn at a much deeper, experiential level through action and discussion as you go about everyday life. The idea is to have a basic understanding of the patterns of a group of people and to approach interaction with them using the right attitude and skills.

Dr. Enoch Wan of Western Seminary calls these two approaches by distinct names. First is the mechanistic approach and the second is the relational transformation approach.[6] Relational transformation is more biblical and more realistic.

To understand relational transformation, you need to understand the relational paradigm. Reality through this lens is described as the relationships between living beings and/or spiritual beings. That is to say, reality includes relationships with God, people, and created spiritual beings (angels or demons).

The biblical example of Acts 16 is a great place to see the interaction between physical reality and relational reality. Paul was called to Macedonia through his relationship with the Lord. After seeing the vision, the missionary band made their way to Philippi and began to teach. An amazing picture is seen in verse 14. It says that the Lord opened Lydia's heart to the things that Paul taught.

Look at the relationships in this narrative.

Paul and his band of gospel workers prayed, served, and worked together. They had what is called a horizontal relationship. "Horizontal" is used to describe relationships between created beings, or those who are on your horizontal plane. Horizontal relationships involve those whom you see face-to-face.

Paul and his group also had a relationship with God the Father, the Son, and the Spirit. That relationship, marked by prayer and direction from God, is called a vertical relationship. "Vertical" is used to describe relationships between created beings and God, who is above.

Using directional terms to describe how God and people interact, you can see how relationships between creator God and the created beings are vertical, while relationships between created beings themselves are horizontal. This model brings up a few important points.

THE NATURE OF RELATIONSHIPS

First, relationships by definition involve two or more beings. What is appropriate for one to bring to the relationship may or may not be appropriate for the other.

Consider the vertical relationship. The Bible talks a lot about how God is involved in human life. The triune God leads, provides, and protects. The Father, Son, and Spirit all play different parts in the plan of salvation. God answers prayer. He controls the physical planet where humans live. He can heal sicknesses without using physical medicines. In some instances he has done other miracles, like giving people the ability to speak and understand languages that they have never used before.

> People in relationship with God are called by his name. They will look for ways to obey the directions that he gives.

When God is in relationship with people, he may choose to do some, all, or none of those things! When people are in relationship with God, their actions are much different. The believer will learn more about God's character, pray, read his words in the Bible, and identify with him through worship and obedience. People in relationship with him are called by his name. They will look for ways to obey the directions that he gives. Those in relationship with God will worship and be a witness to his activity in their life.

God leads, protects, and provides, including the important provision of salvation. This is the nature of God's vertical relationship with people. People enter the relationship with faith, prayer, worship, and obedience. These are the defining features of a relationship with God. The relationship is two-sided and both entities bring something unique.

Horizontal relationships can also be marked by the necessity of different, appropriate responses to each other. A child and his father have a relationship, but they have different roles and responsibilities.

A woman and her elderly mother also have distinct roles and actions.

On the other hand, two friends of the same age that are not related may have a relationship that does not include distinctions. They both can interact freely within their cultural understanding of friendship and bring the same actions and patterns to the relationship. The relationship is vital and important, and both people have the same sense of engagement. Each horizontal interaction will have distinct expectations and responsibilities.

ALL RELATIONSHIPS AREN'T HEALTHY

The second fact of the relational model is that relationships are not universally healthy or appropriate.

Stressing the importance of relationships does not imply that all relationships are beneficial. Some are healthy, and some are not. Some relationships foster growth and maturity in the people involved, and some do not. Some relationships follow the outlines of God's word, and others do not.

> God opens and closes hearts through his vertical relationship with each person.

Unhealthy vertical relationships could include idolatry, or the worship of false gods. In that case it may appear there is a relationship, but it is not valid or healthy.

Similarly, an unhealthy horizontal relationship could include crime, abuse, or codependency. The fact that there is a relationship does not mean it is a healthy one. It is necessary to recognize the central importance of interactive and positive relationships in understanding life.

VERTICAL RELATIONSHIPS ARE UNIQUE

Vertical relationships do not always follow the same patterns. God is very creative and wise. He knows the best way to interact with each person because he made everyone. For that reason, he does not always involve himself the same way with two people, even if those people are involved with one another.

As an example of this, consider the simple case of evangelism. Paul preached the message of salvation to many people in the book of Acts. Lydia's response was not only to Paul, but also to the triune God who had opened her heart to the things spoken by Paul (Acts 16:14). Some of those who hear the gospel will respond because God opens their hearts. Others will not respond. A change in human technique is not necessarily going to make it so that everyone responds!

God is at work to open the hearts of those who receive his message. The human tendency is to think that there is a definite method or technique that will make individual communication more effective. There are ways for clarity in communication, but you have to recognize that God opens and closes hearts through his vertical relationship with each person.

TRANSFORMATION HAPPENS THROUGH SYNCING

One final point is that the bond of human or divine relationship is where you will see transformation take place. Consider these key biblical passages about change and growth.

"Come now, let us reason together, says the Lord: though your sins are like scarlet they shall be as white as snow (Isa. 1:18)." The path to salvation includes interaction – reasoning and conversation with the God of creation.

"Be kind to one another, tenderhearted, forgiving one another as God in Christ forgave you (Eph. 4:32)." God calls on you to shape your relationships with each other after the model of his relational involvement. As he forgave, so you forgive. As he showed kindness, you are called to kindness.

"But grow in the grace and knowledge of our Lord and Savior Jesus Christ (2 Pet. 3:18)." God calls you to not only recognize and understand that he loves you, but to grow based on his kind and gracious interaction. Knowing him changes you – as an individual and in relationships with other people.

Take a look at this graphic, which shows the vertical and horizontal relationships that have been introduced.

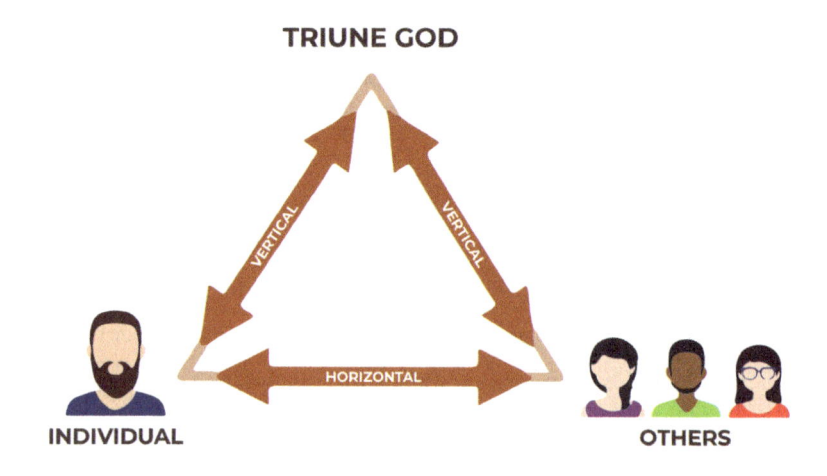

TRIUNE GOD

VERTICAL   VERTICAL

HORIZONTAL

INDIVIDUAL   **OTHERS**

You can see that each person has a relationship with God and other people. The relationship with God is vertical, while relationships with others are horizontal.

ANALYZING RELATIONSHIPS

Besides the biblical perspective, you can also look at relationships through the lens of modern social science. Authors Balswick, King, and Reimer help describe the elements of human relationships.[7] Another recent author, Natalie Kim, discusses a similar analysis in her doctoral studies.[8]

Summarizing these authors, the following are key elements that define relationships.

GRACE AS A FOCAL POINT

In this case, grace means a positive intent or a desire to do what is best for the other person. This is important in all situations, but especially when forgiveness is needed. In the absence of positive intent, the relationship will consist of people who are only interested in their own well-being. In Christian terms, this is not a healthy relationship. Forgiveness and seeking the best for each other is part of a relationship based on grace.

RECIPROCITY

Relationships operate in two directions. Each party will affect the other and be affected by the other. Those impacts will happen in different ways. A father benefits from the joy of watching his child grow while the child benefits from the food, protection, and provision that come from the father. Over time in a healthy relationship, the expressions of each person will change. What does not change is the simple truth that relationships are reciprocal.

THE NATURE OF BEINGS

Relational patterns are formed between beings. In other words, the particular character and role of the creator or created beings will affect the kind of relational patterns that they might form. Horizontal relational interactions are affected by the genders, ages, and social positions of the people involved. Vertical relationships are affected as people relate either appropriately or inappropriately to the Father, Son, and Spirit.

CULTURAL EXPECTATIONS

The cultural patterns of a group of people will strongly influence the kind of relationship that is formed between group members. There are particular cultural expectations for patterns of behavior between men and women, elderly and youth, leaders and followers, and more.

COVENANT EXPECTATIONS

Cultural expectations may include legal or covenantal relationships. A married couple, for instance, will have patterns that are related to the rights and privileges of their national legal system. Covenantal relational patterns could include legal protections at work or in medical situations. Other national legal systems may have a different set of laws that affect horizontal and vertical relationships.

CONTEXT

Relationships are affected by the context in which they take place. Familial relationships will have patterns that are different from those with school friends, romantic partners, business associates, or church pastors.

CLOSENESS/INTIMACY

The level of emotional or physical closeness between people is also a relational element that varies from one culture to another. It takes a good deal of trust to let someone below the surface of your life. Crimes of passion or deception are especially horrible because they are abuses of the closeness that takes place in an intimate relationship.

INFLUENCE

Influence is the last element in understanding relationship as an organizing principle for intercultural ministry. The questions are, "What kind of influence is exerted by the relationship? Who does it benefit?" One employer might seek to empower and build up employees, using his influence for their growth and development. Another manager might only want to influence the profits of their company, and not seek any benefit for the employees. Recognizing the kind of influence that is present and the beneficiary of that influence is an important element in understanding the nature of relational patterns.

THE INTERACTION

This is a book about people who know God working to bring others into a relationship with him. This is a book about what it looks like to leave one's homeland and move into another part of the world where language and behavior is different. This book also speaks to those who receive people from another culture. As people move from culture to culture, keep the focus on relationships instead of seeing ministry as some sort of technique.

> The particular character and role of the creator or created beings will affect the kind of relational patterns that they might form.

When you think about relationships, you almost naturally become more flexible and more likely to shift according to the realities of the people you are talking to. You recognize that people interact differently based on many possible factors – age, gender, educational level, profession, and family interaction, to name a few. If you think of ministry as a technique, you will always use the same pattern to draw close and communicate with people. If you look at life and ministry through the lens of relationship, you will keep your eyes on the final goal, which is helping people grow in a relationship with the Lord. Through this process, you will find yourself shifting your flexibility in terms of how you interact with those people. Relationships are naturally able to change and grow. Methodological ministry, on the other hand, seeks to fit all people into the same pattern.

What is the connection between the idea of syncing and the idea of relationship? Research has shown that people take great joy in syncing with someone. Humans cherish the connection that is created when their brain waves connect with another. Think about the English idiomatic expressions that describe syncing. The following phrases all speak to this reality.

"We were really tracking!"
"We are on the same page!"
"Great minds think alike."

The same is true in vertical relationships, too, though your syncing with God is not an interaction between equals as it is in horizontal relationships.

"Come, now, let us reason together (Isa. 1:18)."

The beatitudes in Matthew 5 celebrate those who are poor in spirit, who mourn, who are gentle, and who are righteous and merciful. A little further on in the passage, you can see that those qualities will glorify God (Matt. 5:16). More powerfully, verse 45 says that these traits are important, "so that you may be sons of your Father who is in heaven." You are called to "be perfect, as your heavenly Father is perfect (Matt. 5:48)." In short, the beatitudes call you to match, or sync, your attitudes, actions, and affections to those of your Father.

SYNCHRONIZATION

In vertical terms, sync with the Lord by spending time with him, learning to value what he values, and asking him to transform you by the renewing of your mind (Rom. 12:2). Through prayer, song, service, reflecting on his word, joining in worship with others, and spiritual discipline, you give God what he deserves. That process of worship leads you to be synchronized with God.

Horizontal relationships sync differently. When you are with your own cultural group, the limiting factor is personal interaction. When people live by the same patterns and get along well, it is fairly natural and simple for hearts and minds to sync together.

When people are from different cultures, syncing is much more challenging. If you struggle over the simplest phrases, how can you communicate so that your minds walk in tandem? When you feel that each cultural pattern you see is somehow strange and uncomfortable, it is unlikely that you will find yourself saying things like "we are on the same page."

The goal of intercultural training is to point you toward the skills and attitudes that will allow you to sync your thoughts and feelings with people whose life patterns are different than yours. It is not that you have to agree with everything in the new culture. The goal is to communicate with as little as possible separating you from those you are sent to. It is powerful to be on the same page in both language and cultural patterns so that you can communicate more clearly.

That kind of synchronization of hearts and minds is not automatic. It grows in relationship with others. It grows with trust between people. It grows when God is at work to open someone's heart to his message. The synchronization of people from distinct cultures grows when mutual understanding and appreciation grows.

The goal you should have for communication is to link your heart and mind with others. No one can teach you how to do that in a specific culture, but you can learn. You will find the tools needed for teaching yourself in the coming chapters.

CHAPTER REVIEW

- What are vertical and horizontal relationships?
- How does syncing work in relationships?
- What are some phrases you use that show how people sync with each other?

PUT IT INTO PRACTICE

- Think about some of your horizontal relationships with friends and family. Do you feel that you are synchronized with them? What examples can you identify that show you are on the same wavelength?
- Think about your relationship with God. What are the most powerful ways that you sync with him?
- How do you envision syncing with neighbors at home or abroad? What can you do to prepare yourself to sync with new people?
- What are some examples you can think of where you felt truly in line with another person? How did that make you feel? Why do you think syncing with others is so important for ministry?

CHAPTER FIVE

Learning Another Culture

※

In the last chapter, it was established that any cross-cultural ministry should focus on relationships more than techniques. As much as you seek to align your thoughts with the people who live in another culture, syncing is not automatic. You have to be deliberate. You have to learn the new culture.

In this chapter, you will read about how to deliberately learn the patterns of another group of people. What are the elements that go into learning an unfamiliar culture? There are two parts to the answer – culture and learning.

WHAT IS CULTURE?

Culture is one of the most interesting ideas that humans have ever started talking about, particularly because it is difficult to put into words. Culture is not something that can be touched or handled. You can't go to the store and buy a gallon or a dozen of it. When talking about culture, you normally discuss practical elements of the idea, but not exactly all of the issues.

Some people speak of culture to refer to politics of their day. For example, you might have heard of "cancel culture." Others speak of culture as a mindset, like the "culture wars" that might separate conservative and liberal political views. Still others use the idea of culture to talk about art and music, for instance the "high culture" that you might find in museums.

Culture incorporates all of the above and much more. If you try to arrange your thoughts to consider each people group and each generation as a unique situation, that becomes too complex to be of practical help. In this book, "culture" means the expected patterns of a group of people that are normal and acceptable to them. These patterns are taught from childhood. In the best case situation, someone who enters a new group of people as an adult will also be pointed toward these patterns.

What do these patterns affect? What are the areas of life that are conditioned by the patterns of the group?

Meals. Clothing. How to raise children. How to work. How to get along with the boss. How to interact with family. Who marries whom. What is really important and what is not a priority. Ideas about where people came from. How to think. How to express emotions. How to sing and dance. How to shape your face for happy situations and for sad situations. How close or far away to stand from others. How time is considered. How to understand seasons of the year and standards of daily living.

> " Culture means the expected patterns of a group of people that are normal and acceptable to them.

Do you get the idea? You can see patterns of thought, feeling and behavior in all areas of life. Can you imagine the chaos and misunderstanding if every individual had to treat each meeting with another person as its own unique circumstance? That would be incomprehensible, confusing, and exhausting! Instead of inventing new standards for all of these different parts of life, culture gives you patterns that you can and should use. There can be some flexibility, but any group of people will be much more comfortable as these accepted patterns are repeated over and over by different members of the group.

When discussing culture, people often only include things like clothing, arts, or food. The reality is that people groups have patterns of thought, emotional display, selling and buying, and so much more. The youngest group members spend an enormous amount of energy and time watching the older group members, especially their parents. As they grow, children learn the patterns of interaction, speech, and involvement with the physical world. Children pick up cues in a variety of places including the home, the place of worship, stores, and school.

The correction that takes place when a child does not follow the norms or expectations of the group is really uncomfortable for them. They learn to do what the group expects in order to avoid the pain of being corrected. Children learn so well that they understand the patterns of their people implicitly. The word "intuition" refers to what is known but does not need to be put into words. What you know intuitively is so deeply planted that you really can't imagine life any other way. The intuitive is natural for that group of people. Another group of people can easily create a different pattern. The patterns of one group of people are not the patterns of another group. That is the reality that leads to a world filled with diverse cultures.

Keep in mind as you read that the word "culture" means patterns. It means the accepted and appropriate ways of dealing with the circumstances of life that a group of people have adopted.

There are two important things to think about concerning this definition of culture. First, if culture is about patterns, is the study of culture all about the differences between cultures? Additionally, if culture is all about patterns that are naturally learned as a child, what does it mean for the person who is moving into a new group of people as an adult?

If culture is life patterns, wouldn't the study of many cultures be the study of differences between the patterns of one group compared to another? The answer is no. For years, the idea of culture was presented as examining the strange customs, traditions, and beliefs of a group of people who lived in some other part of the world. It is no wonder that for many people, the concept of culture might be tied to the idea of cataloging the distinctions between different groups of people.

> The word "intuition" refers to what is known but does not need to be put into words. What you know intuitively is so deeply planted that you really can't imagine life any other way. The intuitive is natural for a group of people.

From a biblical perspective, humans have more things in common than things that separate. Even the patterns of food or clothing can be viewed from the perspective of commonalities rather than solely focusing on differences.

The following chart shows how to understand culture as what is in common before identifying points of diversity.

HUMAN CHARACTERISTIC	ONE CULTURE	ANOTHER CULTURE
The need to eat	Frequent consumption of red meat	Frequent consumption of vegetables
The need for protection from the elements	Clothing that is formal and expensive	Clothing that is informal, casual, minimal
The need for interaction with leadership	Leaders are given extra liberty and recognition	Leaders give direction and oversight but aren't treated differently
The need for prioritization of work activities	Prioritization of buildings, infrastructure, and military	Prioritization of food, education, and medical care
The need for common thought processes	Thinking starts with the big idea and works toward application	Thinking starts with many life examples and works toward drawing conclusions
The need for trust in communication	Trust in more cognitive and objective communication	Trust in more emotional expression
The need to understand humanity and life purpose	Belief that humans are a happy accident	Belief that humans were created and designed by God

No one can teach you about a culture because there are just too many patterns that differ from one group of people to another. You can, however, look at that in a different way. You can start with the point of view that all humans have the same set of basic life issues, and then recognize that there are a wide variety of ways to address those issues. As you read this book, think in terms of what unites you and then look at the range of responses that various groups have for meeting those challenges.

How can an adult move into a new culture? Children learn the patterns of their culture through watching, receiving correction, and praise. What about adults? How do adults who move to a new place learn those cultural patterns? To answer that question, move to this chapter's second major question.

WHAT IS LEARNING?

This chapter is titled simply, "learning another culture." You have read about culture. Now turn your attention to what is involved with learning.

It is not as simple as it seems, especially when the subject matter is as wide-ranging as culture. Culture can be extremely subtle. Think about all of the messages that can be expressed through minute differences in smiles. Culture can also be blunt and obvious. Not everyone around the world would wear a religious veil, for instance. In any case, whether you are moving to live among other people or welcoming someone from a different culture, you will have to learn cultural patterns that you are not familiar with.

With new technology, researchers have discovered new details about human learning. Author Stanislas Dehaene gives a great overview of the process of learning.[9] His description stems from technical research into brain functions that only recently have been physically possible. Tools like Magnetic Resonance Imaging (MRI) allow researchers to see how the various parts of the brain work together in different life circumstances.

Another great resource for understanding the process of learning, especially as it occurs in the physical brain, is Zaretta Hammond's book, Culturally Responsive Teaching and the Brain.[10] Much like Dehaene and other authors, this book looks at human learning from the perspective of the physical makeup and hormonal influences of the brain. What makes Hammond's work especially helpful is the application to multicultural learning situations. Though her work speaks specifically of learning done by children, it is still useful for adults.

In light of these two authors, what is true about learning a new culture? The points that follow are adapted from recent publications and summarize insights into how people learn.

1. Humans learn best when there is a mental model, or schema. Culture learning is more effective when adding details to overarching theories of culture and education. Learning is best when you can see enough samples that allow you to search for patterns. When it comes to culture learning, this is great news because culture is related to the life patterns of a group of people. People learn by noticing those patterns and the appropriate responses to those patterns.
2. Humans learn best when receiving feedback. Culture is best learned when you are allowed to identify issues and work to minimize errors. This can be tricky because many cultures of the world are not comfortable with direct negative feedback. Still, people learn by hearing what worked and what did not. That feedback loop is a key part of the learning process.
3. Humans learn best through trial and error. Culture is learned by acting on possibilities and eliminating those that cause a negative reaction. There is a creative side to the

best culture learners because they are not afraid to try new things and see what reaction ensues.
4. Humans learn best when there are rewards. There are inherent rewards to learning culture. The human brain is bathed in hormones, some that are pleasant and some that are unpleasant. When there is success in learning a task in a new culture, there are hormonal rewards in the form of dopamine release. Other intrinsic rewards for culture learning come from the joy of syncing mental functions with other people.
5. Humans learn best when the number of possible variables is restricted. Learning a culture by analyzing one stimulus at a time is much more effective than trying to gauge the impact of a whole scene.
6. Humans learn best when creating a hypothesis, or guess, and then monitoring to see what happens. Analysis, observation, and comparison are essential tools that give confidence in the learning process.
7. Humans learn best when following proven methods. There are at least four trusted elements in culture learning:
   - Awareness of similarities and differences
   - Authentic relationships between the learner and a local teacher
   - A cognitive model for learning that leads to action
   - A community that is safe and encouraging

> Culture can be extremely subtle. Culture can also be blunt and obvious. You will learn cultural patterns that are not familiar.

There is a lot of personal risk in the process of learning a culture. Following tried-and-true methods will minimize that risk.

No one can teach you a new culture – there are too many variables to identify and model. You can still learn! Learning takes place...

> ...with a mental model of the concepts of culture, learning, and the specific life elements involved in the new culture.
>
> ...when you are careful to nurture the attitudes that help you to learn, which will make you comfortable and confident in the process.
>
> ...when there is a community involved, both to model the expected patterns of a group of people and to give feedback.
>
> ...when there are specific skills identified to help you observe, adjust, and adapt to the patterns you see.

Consider this powerful situation. There was a trainer leading a workshop in a culture that he had never before visited. The trainer was practicing self-directed learning principles within the community and the school where he was working. At the end of the two-week training, one of the local members made an interesting comment. "We have loved the ideas you have shared, but we are bothered because you are a liar."

You can imagine the confusion on the trainer's face! "Why do you think I'm lying?" he asked. The trainee responded, "We have had expats live in our community for years, and they never understood us like you do. When you say that you have never been here before, we don't believe you. You must have lived here for many years to know how to work with us so well!" This level of synchronization should be the goal for all culture learners.

CHAPTER REVIEW

- What is culture? What is learning?
- Why is it important to identify commonalities before differences?
- What is an example of a human characteristic that presents itself differently among cultures?

PUT IT INTO PRACTICE

- What things are ingrained in your culture? What actions or patterns can you identify that you have always followed and were taught by your parents?
- How can you develop the style of culture learning that was discussed in this chapter? How can you grow toward an intercultural life that syncs with people who come from radically different backgrounds?
- Go through the best practices of learning and give an example of how you can put each into practice when you are in an unfamiliar culture.

CHAPTER SIX

A Mental Model

✦

As you start to build a mental model to help your adaptation and adjustment into an unfamiliar culture, here is a very brief review of what has been discussed so far.

- Chapter 1 introduced the journey. It is not a physical trip, but a journey within. The mission is to connect your mind and heart with the minds and hearts of people from other cultures.
- Chapter 2 was an overview of the big purpose. Jesus' church will include a group of every tribe, language, people, and nation. Jesus is building his church now, and that gives you the opportunity to grow in your ability to interact well with people of many cultures.
- Chapter 3 discussed the invisible influences that shape you and that shape culture. One of the highlights of intercultural life and work is growing to the point where your thoughts and expressions synchronize with others. When that deep level of communication takes place, it is easier to talk about God and his kingdom without encountering avoidable hindrances in the process.
- Chapter 4 was a closer look at syncing through the lens of relationship. Seeing relationships in vertical terms (between

God and creation) and in horizontal terms (between created beings) is key to intercultural ministry.
- Chapter 5 described definitions of "culture" and "learning." For you to build healthy relational patterns that permit a flow of communication, it is necessary to think carefully about how you learn to interact with other cultures. That is the part of life that no one can teach you, but you can learn!

Since Babel (Gen. 11:1-9), humans have had to adjust to a world with diverse cultural patterns. Though the vocabulary of those interactions has changed, there are an almost infinite number of factors that shape the patterns of life for any one group of people. Experience, geography, history, and power, are just a few of the possible differences between people. Thinking about these help you realize how diverse the cultures of the world really are.

These diverse ways of life actually have much in common. When you look at different cultures, you start to realize that they grew from different responses to the same human realities. Everybody needs to eat, but how that need is met can happen in a variety of ways. Everyone needs to work as individuals within a community. How groups respond to individual and community leadership is what differs between cultures. Even more examples include exchanging goods and services, teaching the next generation, prioritizing tasks, or communicating non-verbally. All of these and much more become the unifying concepts under which a range of diverse responses can be seen in the world.

In this chapter you will be introduced to a tool that helps to develop the concept of seeing humanity first through unifying factors and then diversity. It is a tool called "The Culture Tree." [11]

Trying to envision and somehow model the concept of culture has been a goal of intercultural educators for years. You could think about many objects to use as a metaphorical representation of culture. Some examples might have the hidden and invisible as an integral part of the model. Others may exemplify that culture comprises many factors, including the superficial preferences.

The problem with other objects, however, is that none is complex enough to represent a life cycle. Trees, though, are different. They live and then die. They respond to issues in their environment, and they are shaped by those influences. Human cultures on this planet face that same predicament. The Culture Tree allows you to see how the pieces of a culture work together while also acknowledging the living, responsive nature of a given tribe, language, people, and nation.

The following is an illustration of The Culture Tree, including nine elements of culture to analyze in terms of unity, then diversity.

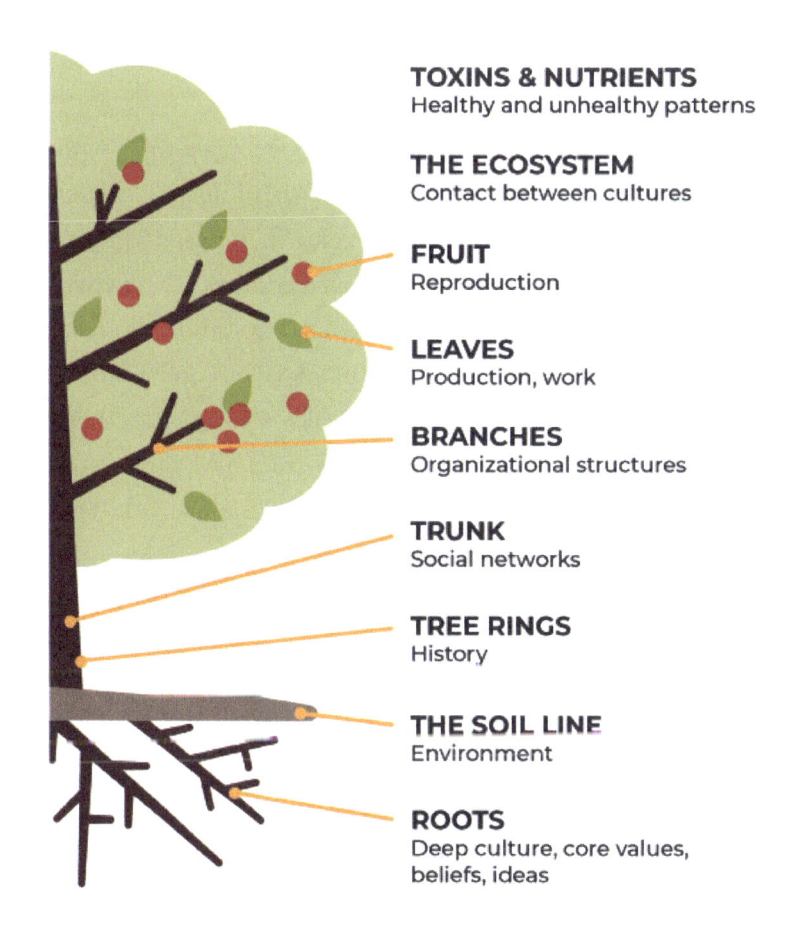

TOXINS & NUTRIENTS
Healthy and unhealthy patterns

THE ECOSYSTEM
Contact between cultures

FRUIT
Reproduction

LEAVES
Production, work

BRANCHES
Organizational structures

TRUNK
Social networks

TREE RINGS
History

THE SOIL LINE
Environment

ROOTS
Deep culture, core values, beliefs, ideas

Think for a moment about the beautiful variety of trees in the world. There are towering Redwoods, Douglas Firs, palm trees in the tropics, and isolated Savannah trees in the dry plains of Africa. You can look at harsh environments and see trees that grow slowly, forever stunted as they develop in the midst of challenging conditions.

> **When you look at different cultures, you start to realize that in many ways they all grew from responses to the same human realities.**

One of the beautiful things about symbolizing cultures with trees is that this picture captures the essence of variation and uniqueness among groups. There are cultures that value their past and others that live for today. There are cultures that have centuries of experience and others that are newly developing. There are some that create elaborate social structures and others that develop a simple collection of family groups. The image of the tree allows you to first think about commonalities by acknowledging all trees have the same parts, and then to address differences by thinking of the many different types of trees.

Take a deeper look at the nine elements of The Culture Tree. For each part of the tree, three important factors will be included: a description of the unifying cultural element, an example of how the patterns are seen in different cultures, and a diagnostic question to help you understand and utilize this knowledge in an unfamiliar culture.

ROOTS

The roots of the tree are arguably the most important for the long-term well-being of the tree. Without the roots, the tree would not exist. An amazing fact is that a high percentage of living matter in a tree is actually buried underground! Up to 40 or 50% of the whole tree is found in its roots.[12] In many cases, chopping or burning a tree will not kill it; as long as the roots remain alive, the tree can regrow.

The roots of The Culture Tree refer to the worldview of a culture. The roots represent the unspoken assumptions, values, and expectations of a group of people.

That image helps you to understand unfamiliar cultures. There is always a network of key ideas, beliefs, and values that one generation teaches to another. Like the roots of a tree, those deeply held beliefs give stability and nourishment to the tree. As values are taught through generations, the culture grows and thrives.

Beliefs are the statements that people see as true even though defining them could be difficult. "We hold these truths to be self-evident," says the United States Declaration of Independence. The statements that follow are considered roots for the American people.

Values tell a group what is right and what is wrong. Values are used as a tool to evaluate what you should and should not do. Groups define what they value, they teach that to coming generations, and they evaluate behaviors on the basis of those values.

One great place to see the values and beliefs of a group of people is the stories, books, and activities that are presented to the children. American children's literature and teaching materials in school will include a number of common themes and stories on topics like self-regulation, being truthful, and justice. If it's taught to those who are young and learning, it will already be a deeply held belief of older generations.

Another factor in the roots of a culture is expected responses. How should you help a friend in need? How should you respond in a car accident? How would you act if you get a job promotion? How do you greet people? The answers to these questions reflect a culture's intuitive behaviors.

All cultures grow from one generation to the next and express the values, beliefs, and expectations of their culture to their children. In a tree, water, nutrients, and stability are the benefits of strong roots. If you think about the analogy of culture, you might realize that strength and nourishment come from the worldview, the values, and beliefs that are found in the cultural roots.

This point is easy to underestimate. How many times in Christian mission or in some other project do people suggest changes to the organizational patterns? Those kinds of "above-the-soil" change rarely have any lasting impact unless accompanied by deeper "root level" change. This is because a culture grows from the roots. If there is a need for change in a group of people, that change will only take place to the degree that it affects the values, expectations, and beliefs of the group. To bring about lasting change, the roots must be in focus.

Jesus used the word "heart" to talk about the invisible part of a person. The Culture Tree uses roots. In any case, real change takes place when those roots or that heart is shaken out of preconceived beliefs, values, and expectations and transformed into godly truths and values. Mission work is not about establishing new social structures. Mission work is about seeing the truths of God's word, the values of God's kingdom, and the expectations that come from seeing God at work in and through his people.

The key question for understanding the roots of a culture is, "What are the values, beliefs, and expected responses to life situations?" This question can be asked to analyze a culture that you are learning, or it can be used deliberately to create the culture you wish to achieve in a company, school, church, or other organization.

SOIL LINE

The soil line is where the roots stop and exposure to the above-ground environment begins. The environment has a significant impact on how the tree grows. The processes of a tree adapt to the weather, location, and other environmental factors of the tree.

In the same way, any pattern of life will reflect realities of the physical environment that surrounds it. A maritime village will have different work and play patterns than a city in the middle of the prairies. Those who live in the mountains have a different way of life from people who live in the Amazon valley basin. The environment shapes daily patterns in a number of ways. Snow plows and their drivers are not a big commodity in Hawaii!

> Just like one cell touches another in a tree trunk, so too one person touches another throughout a culture. They are all connected.

It can be more subtle, too. In an interesting article about wheat-growing societies compared with rice-growers, author Michaeleen Doucleff suggests that rice requires communities to work together, but wheat can be grown in solitary fields.[13] Rice, in other words, needs a group working together to maximize yield for everyone's sake. Wheat farmers can work independently of their neighbors. This illustration is not only an indication of the physical environment but it also reflects the core values of individualism and community cohesion.

Another way that the physical environment plays an important role in culture is through the stories, songs, and fables of a people and the land where they live. Think of the songs or fables that you learned as a child. Some of those had to do with places around you – a mountain or a lake, for example. Those stories tie a people to their heritage and to their land. Culture and the environment are closely associated.

If you are learning an unfamiliar culture, pay attention to the land. Do the people live on an island? Do they come from valleys between isolated mountains? Besides learning the cultural patterns of the place where you might be moving, think about the immigrants who live in your homeland. What kinds of land and physical environment did they come from? Answering these questions will almost certainly give you insight into the life patterns of the people.

The key questions for understanding the soil line are, "What physical environment do the people live in or come from? How does that physical environment affect their life patterns?"

TRUNK

One of the most fascinating things about trees is that the cells inside a tree are interconnected so extensively that a drop of liquid appearing in the highest leaves started its journey in the roots. Almost no water or nutrients of a tree are absorbed by the leaves; practically all of it starts a long journey from cell to cell through what is called the vascular tissue. This journey doesn't stop until it arrives where it is needed, perhaps even in the highest crown of that tree.[12]

While there are a lot of factors involved in moving water "from roots to shoots," the important thing to know is that the cells of a tree trunk are all connected. One cell touches another that touches another. Water moves up the tree – against gravity – by moving through a network of cells. The trunk illustrates two important lessons for understanding a culture.

First, the people in a culture are interrelated. They network together in ways that allow for the movement of information, ideas, and opinions. Just like one cell touches another in a tree trunk, so too one person touches another throughout a culture. They are all connected.

Additionally, all other elements of culture are correlated. The economy, values, government, schools, entertainment, and more are all cohesive in a culture. Even though there are different approaches used to break down elements of culture into understandable parts, all parts are interwoven.

The network that exists across a culture impacts the people and the actions they take. This connection of people and cultural elements is an important part of comprehending The Culture Tree.

The relationships between people are particularly dynamic and important. While you interact within your network of peers, you are limited in your sheer ability to know others. The Dunbar number suggests that each person can only successfully know about 150 people.[14] Communicologist Donald Smith suggests that those 150 people are not all equally involved.[5] You have a core group of people with whom you have intimate conversations, another with whom you share daily life, and another with whom you interact with at a distance. Outside of those levels is the large group with whom you share very little but you know by name.

When looking at networks in a culture, there are two points of view.

The first perspective considers interaction between people. Who gets to know whom? What are the barriers to interactive relationships? Do men speak freely with women? How do children interact? Are there national, racial, or ethnic factors that limit networking in some way?

The second point of view focuses on the interaction between organizational levels of The Culture Tree. How does the government interact with the family? How do schools help to prepare a new generation of people? What teamwork is there between the factory and the hospital? Analyzing these questions helps to identify the networking elements within a culture.

GROWTH RINGS

It is hard to think of trees without also thinking of the beautiful color, texture, and markings of a piece of wood. Among the features of wood, the alternating series of lighter and darker rings that appear in a cross-section is especially beautiful.

Those rings are growth rings, laid down year after year as the tree develops. With those rings you can see the history of the tree. They may indicate a period of especially good growth, a forest fire that damaged some of the bark, or seasons of drought. Tree rings tell where the tree has been and how long it has been alive. The simple fact is that the tree's history is recorded in the growth rings of its trunk.

Trees are shaped by their history. In the same way, of all the forces that shape a culture, it is hard to underestimate the power of history. The history that has an impact is not cleaned up or reinterpreted for people from other lands. It is raw, full of emotion and personal involvement. It is the story of the past as they tell it to each other. It is not only the details of the battle or the economic collapse, it is the story of how someone's uncle or grandfather coped with that downturn. It is not just the development of an illness, it is the story of friends and family who died or were forever changed by the outbreak.

Those stories of the people are not told for the sake of the past generations. They are told in order to shape the hearts and minds of young people. Knowing where a group came from, in their own words, is vital to understanding their culture. Where do patterns of life, belief, and thought come from? They come from generations of tradition and stories of the past told in personal and societal terms.

Learning the history of a people as they tell it is a gift and a privilege. Depending on the people involved, you will hear of injustices, trials, difficulties, triumphs, and defeats. You will hear of those who are considered the heroes and those who are the villains. You will hear of the leaders that are admired and those who are reviled.

The people will not tell this story to just anyone. Those who hear of the past are trusted to receive it without judgment. What social scientists call the "ability to withhold judgment" is a necessary skill for receiving these stories. Gaining the trust of the people through life interaction is part of being able to hear their history. One of the biggest reasons that people hear these stories is simply because they are together. If your busy schedule pulls you out of all activities as soon as they are finished, you will rarely have the long talks that lead to in-depth discussion of the history of the group.

> **Of all the forces that shape a culture, it's hard to underestimate the power of history.**

If you are entering another culture as an expatriate, your starting point is learning. You should read the official histories, visit the museums, and watch the films that portray the history of the people as told by them. You can ask your new neighbors and colleagues about what you have seen, though it is not likely that they will share openly at first. You must listen and make yourself available for later conversation. When you least expect it, you will have conversations that enlighten you to their past as they understand it.

If you are receiving people into your own land, follow that same long and slow entry ramp; however, you should spend time learning of their culture and asking why they have moved to a new place. Awareness of current events in their homeland will help you to better understand their patterns of life. Once you start to get an idea of their history, you will see how their culture was formed. You can also give them the blessing of telling them your own personal and cultural history.

The key questions for this level of The Culture Tree are, "What are some significant pieces of the history of the culture you are working with? What are some significant pieces of their personal history?"

BRANCHES

The branches of a tree support the leaves, which are vital for nutrition. Look at how branches extend from the trees around you. In some cases, they are in a circle at the same height on the trunk. In other cases the branches disperse at various heights and directions. The organization of branches ensures maximum sunlight exposure for the leaves.

In the same way, the organizations of any culture are varied and structured in the way that the people group thinks is best. Consider the national governments around the world. There are democracies, monarchies, cultures that prefer one strong leader, and others that seek a consensus of leaders.

When you enter a new culture or welcome people from a different culture, it is important to learn about their national government system. It is likely that expected leadership and organizational patterns in non-governmental systems will be similar. Churches in the United States often look to both an elder board or board of trustees for most situations and rely on the pastoral staff for teaching. This is similar to the relationship between the Executive Branch and Legislative Branch in the federal and state governments. This structure feels normal to church members from the US. That same structure may be confusing to people from other countries. Churches in other parts of the world, for example, will likely prefer that the pastor has the stronger voice and that any elders take a less dominant role.

In both cases, those churches see themselves as reflecting a biblical model in leadership, and they refer to cultural and biblical examples that support their organization. In any culture, people adapt to the leadership patterns that are in place and often duplicate those patterns in businesses, churches, and other organizations.

Beside the organizational structures, there is another element of leadership that social researcher Geert Hofstede calls "power distance."[15] This speaks to the preferred relationship between leaders and their people. A high power distance culture will prefer that leaders be recognized with special privileges, titles, and rights. It is important to know that this is not just the leader's preference. The people also prefer these methods of honoring and respecting leaders.

A low power distance relationship between leader and people means that leaders are not recognized with those special perks. In these cases, the leader is just one of the people whose tasks involve management of others, but there is no additional privilege.

As you get involved with an unfamiliar culture – whether you have moved into a new part of the world or you have welcomed people from elsewhere – the question to answer is, "What are the patterns of organizational structure in government, school, church, and business?"

LEAVES

For a tree, everything depends on its ability to absorb sunlight and carbon dioxide, and to fabricate biological chemicals. There are a lot of structures and forces that are working to complete these vital tasks, but the majority of this work occurs in the leaves. You don't need an in-depth technical description of the process to understand that the leaves provide a cultural parallel for work.

It turns out that cultures, like trees, have certain places and structures where work is done. There are patterns to how work is completed, who does it, what is done, and where it takes place. Moving outside of those patterns can be confusing and even damaging to the members of that culture.

Geert Hofstede offers insights into the nature of work done by various cultures.[15] Using the stereotypical roles that men and women take in some western nations, he calls these work patterns "masculine" and "feminine."

> In order for a culture to continue, there has to be consistency in what they pass down.

A masculine work culture will prioritize work that produces construction, military, and infrastructure. The focus of the culture will revolve around new highways, new buildings, strong factory presence, and a strong military to protect against outside threats. The feminine cultural patterns prioritize softer production. Things like education, health care, and nutrition programs will be more in focus for these cultures.

Like all parts of The Culture Tree, it is rare for any culture to exclusively perform masculine or feminine work. Reality is a mixed bag that includes both. Still, it is important to consider how a culture prioritizes its work. Questions to represent the leaves are, "What are the preferred outcomes of work? Which is most sought after – military and factory output or health and education?"

FRUIT

How do species of trees continue reproducing generation after generation? They create seeds and fruit that are the starting point for new trees to come. Without reproduction and fruit, the species would cease to exist.

The continuation of any culture is carried out through the next generation. Considering this fact, you can analyze the patterns that each generation leaves for the next. In other words, what are the objects, organizations, and lessons that are passed down to the children?

Similar to all of The Culture Tree, there is both unity and diversity in this question. The unity is in the fact that each generation will leave values, patterns, and objects for future generations. You can see diversity in what those particular objects, values, and patterns are.

One group may leave strong education and a tradition of work that creates new jobs for each generation. Others may put the emphasis on keeping the family intact or leaving a monetary inheritance. There are cultural patterns at work in both of those extremes, and many cultures will be somewhere in the middle.

In order for a culture to continue, there has to be consistency in what they pass down. The key question to ask as you work in an unfamiliar culture is, "What does one generation leave to the next?"

TOXINS AND NUTRIENTS

Trees have a variety of biochemical pathways that they use to survive and grow. Each tree requires certain nutrients that are necessary for it to thrive. Since trees are not the only object in the environment, there are also many elements that could bring it harm.

In the same way, each culture must screen influences that are healthy and unhealthy. Some things can be positive to a culture, others can harm it. The opposite may be true for a different culture.

This lesson can be seen in a small rural Bible school in Mexico. One day, a missionary leader began to feel that the group needed to work on developing the skill of private Bible study and prayer. The leader was thinking of the value and power of this time in his own culture in the United States.

He made the individual decision to add a time of private Bible study to the daily schedule for all of the staff and students. He meant for this time to be carried out in the privacy of their own room. When he announced it, he thought it would be well received. He was shocked to find stiff opposition from the students and staff alike.

He asked them why it seemed they did not want additional time for Bible study and prayer. They quickly shared that while they loved the idea of additional quiet time, they did not want to sit alone in their room. Their suggestion was to have this personal devotion time, but while in the same room as their peers. In this situation, their cultural nutrient was togetherness where the missionary's nutrient was alone time. This nutrient for the leader was a toxin for the people.

> **Each part of the tree is distinct and yet they all come together to represent a group of people.**

What are the factors that foster personal and corporate growth in your new culture? What are the factors that cause destruction and result in an unhealthy lifestyle? Learning to identify a new culture's toxins and nutrients will help you to better adapt and adjust to the patterns of the group.

Taking the time to recognize your own culture's nutrients and toxins is also important. People rarely stop to consider how they are influenced by the patterns that have become habitual. Those habits form expectations across cultures. At some point you will think that what is good for you and your culture must also be good for neighbors from distinct cultural backgrounds. This is simply not true. Each set of patterns includes actions and influences that are positive and health-sustaining along with those that are negative and harmful.

Take some time to dwell on these influences for yourself and try to identify what they might be for someone else. What are the toxins and nutrients for other cultures? Why might these be important to acknowledge?

ECOSYSTEM

Trees live in all kinds of environments and those environments produce all kinds of life. The tree in a temperate forest is surrounded by other kinds of trees, vines, shrubs, and animals. Roots of one tree can interact with roots of another to give mutual support – both physical and biochemical. It turns out that the old saying "can't see the forest for the trees" carries a good bit of truth. The forest itself can be healthy and productive beyond just the growth of the individual trees.

On the other hand, there are trees in savannas around the world that are separated by hundreds of meters from the nearest tree. There is virtually no interaction between trees, but much interaction with other living creatures in that ecosystem. The grasses, soil, fungi, and burrowing animals all influence those lone trees scattered across the prairie.

To put this into cultural terms, cultures are influenced and aided by surrounding national or international cultures. For many cultures, another culture may play a foundational role. The ecosystem of any culture is the point where it connects with other cultures.

As you enter an unfamiliar culture or welcome those from other cultures, the question to answer is, "How do the cultural patterns that you are learning interact with other cultures?"

PUTTING IT ALL TOGETHER

The Culture Tree model allows you to see all the elements of a culture and how they interact. Each part of the tree is distinct and yet they all come together to represent a group of people. The values, beliefs, and ideas of a culture show up in every part of their tree.

This chapter concludes with an overview of the concepts that a number of intercultural studies have identified over the past few decades. The roots of the culture relate to both unity of humankind and the diversity of individual patterns. In the chart that follows you will see short descriptions of some of these points of unity, the diversity within them, and references where you can learn more. This is a small sample of the large number of intercultural dimensions that have been identified.

The interesting thing about this listing of cultural dynamics is that you may often see them as differences to be navigated. In this case, start by understanding the things that humans have in common. As you understand those commonalities, you can better understand the unity that you find in the midst of diverse approaches to life.

POINT OF UNITY	ONE EXTREME	ANOTHER EXTREME	REFERENCE FOR STUDY
How the group interacts with the individual	Individualism	Social collectivism	Geert Hofstede[27]
How the group interacts with the leaders	High power distance	Low power distance	Geert Hofstede[27]
The priority outcomes of the culture	Focus on military, infrastructure, and factory production	Focus on education, health, and nutrition	Geert Hofstede[27]
Comfort in the midst of uncertainty	High uncertainty avoidance	Low uncertainty avoidance	Geert Hofstede[27]

POINT OF UNITY	ONE EXTREME	ANOTHER EXTREME	REFERENCE FOR STUDY
Degree of individual freedom to seek pleasure	Self-restraint	Indulgence	Geert Hofstede[27]
Time window for understanding events	Long-term orientation	Short-term orientation	Geert Hofstede[27]
Thinking patterns	Look for universal truths	Look for particular application in a given context	Fons Trompenaars and Charles Hampden-Turner[16]
Relationship between society and nature	Mankind in control of nature	Mankind lets nature take its course	Fons Trompenaars and Charles Hampden-Turner[16]
Feelings and culture	Emotion is trustworthy	Cognitive logic is trustworthy	Fons Trompenaars and Charles Hampden-Turner[16]
Implicit or explicit communication styles	Listening to the air	Making the implicit explicit	Erin Meyer[17]
The etiquette of feedback	Negative feedback given freely	Stated evaluations are kept positive	Erin Meyer[17]
Communication patterns – verbal or contextual	Highly verbal	Highly contextual	Edwin Hoffman and Arjan Verdooren[18]
Communication patterns overall	Assertive	Passive	Andy Molinsky[19]
Interaction in group work	Competitive	Cooperative	David Livermore[20]
Geographic background	Clusters from one part of the world	Cultural clusters from other parts of the world	David Livermore[20]
Thought patterns	High context	Low context	Richard Nisbett[21]

CHAPTER REVIEW

- What is The Culture Tree?
- Why are the elements of The Culture Tree important to learn?
- What elements of The Culture Tree would you see quickly in a new culture? What would take time to learn?

PUT IT INTO PRACTICE

- How do you see yourself using The Culture Tree in your new environment? How could you use The Culture Tree in your home environment?
- Create a Culture Tree with examples for your own culture. Create a Culture Tree for a new culture.
- Talk with a friend about their observations of your patterns. What things can you identify that are ingrained in your lifestyle?

CHAPTER SEVEN

The Languages of Culture

⚜

Learning a culture is easy enough that babies and young children do it all the time! If this is true, then why are you taking the time to read a book about it?

The learning that children do is intuitive. They learn it as they learn basic motor functions, so the cultural patterns and habits become second nature. Learning to see similarities and differences and then deliberately replacing habits to fit into an unfamiliar culture is quite different. The adult has different motivations, resources, and skills for counterintuitive learning.

In this chapter you will find an in-depth look at the skill of observation. As you observe, you will be able to identify relational patterns.

To learn a culture, you must observe the culture. If you can't describe the lifestyle and thoughts that your new neighbors have, how can you hope to shift your behavior to adopt those patterns?

One of the strongest tools for developing the skill of observation comes from Dr. Donald Smith in his textbook Creating Understanding.[5] That tool has been adapted for this book. It is called The Languages of Culture and it emphasizes twelve different forms of human communication. Think about these in detail.

SPEECH

Words matter. What is meant to be communicated through the words that people choose? How does one generation shift the meaning of some words compared to an earlier generation? Which words are repeated frequently and which ones are seldom used?

When you learn to observe at the level of language, you should listen to the content of the message and the way that the message is constructed. This involves learning grammar, vocabulary, and emphasis given by word choice.

This can be illustrated with the way that mothers in the United States will often call for their children. If the problem is not urgent, a mom might call, "John!" almost all the time. If John was in trouble for something, he knows about it before he ever gets close to her because she will probably yell, "John Raymond Smith!" The emphasis of using his full name is reserved for certain situations.

As you learn the language of other people, pay attention to the words that are used in normal circumstances and in unusual situations. The way people communicate verbally is an important pattern in any culture.

WRITING

Written language is not just spoken language in writing. It obviously has some overlap, but written language needs its own observation.

What words are preferred in different kinds of writing? What grammatical rules apply to writing that may not be important in spoken language? What are the ways that written words are used in various situations like ads, textbooks, or news reports? In the internet age, how is written language used in different digital media? How do people write on social media? How do people write to each other? The point again is that you are looking for patterns. The patterns of written communication vary greatly from speaking and also vary among formats of writing.

OBJECTS

People on planet earth greatly value material objects. You could make many assumptions about a person based on the make of the car they drive or the clothing brand they wear. The impression that an object gives in one culture may be different than the same object in another culture. The value of each item in a culture is a major part of its habits and traditions.

> To learn a culture, you must observe a culture. If you can't understand your neighbors, how can you hope to shift your life to their patterns?

The person in an unfamiliar culture can fit in faster or slower depending on their skill of observing and adapting to the use of objects. Clothing, vehicles, tools, instruments, furniture in the house or office, toys, books, and more give insight into the cultural norms and history.

NUMBERS

Numbers may not immediately strike you as an element of culture. On second thought, you might be able to see how certain numbers play a huge role in habits and traditions of a people group. Learning to observe and understand the uses of numbers can be a major bridge to a new culture.

Think of 666. Based on its use in the Bible, this number is often viewed as unlucky or Satanic, but elsewhere it could mean nothing. Think of medical uses of numbers, or how economic reports use numbers. How a culture chooses to weigh and measure will surely have an impact on how life is lived there. Buying a kilo of sugar is not the same as buying a pound!

There are other subtleties in the use of numbers. For instance, what order is common for days, months, and years when writing them as numbers? Would June 10 be 10/6 or 6/10? From culture to culture that may change.

How many days are in a week? While the seven-day week is found around the world, it is used differently. If today is Tuesday and you want to meet a friend next Tuesday you might say, "See you in 8 days," in some parts of the world. In these cultures it is common to count both the first day and the last. Other cultures might only count the last day.

Learning to observe these nuances in the use of numbers will go a long way in helping to better understand and be understood in an unfamiliar culture.

SOUNDS

What are the sirens, songs, and tones of voice that carry significant meaning? For many cultures, sound and song is filled with rich history. Observing these patterns of sound will help you better live and work with new people.

Some sounds are hard to miss. A call to prayer or a rock concert, for example, will be noticeable by the whole community. Other sounds are less apparent. Think about the tone of voice that a parent might use with a child. Along those lines, every parent on the planet at one time or another has probably said to their child, "You will not talk to me with that tone of voice!"

What are repeated sounds used in cultural music? What are the intonations that a speaker will use to signal sarcasm? What about common ringtones or text announcements? When you observe sound patterns you can get an idea of importance, style, and relationship in a particular culture.

BODY LANGUAGE

Communication is more than just talking. You might smile, nod, shake your head, or cross your arms to communicate how you feel. Body language is a key element of communication and the patterns for expected body language vary among cultures. It is through observation that you can know what a given signal or gesture might mean in another culture.

People use hand gestures to punctuate and reinforce speech. They use facial expressions to give clues about their reaction to a given situation. You constantly use your body to indicate emotion and communicate messages without speaking.

Deaf communities around the world primarily use their body to communicate. Their elaborate languages use face, hands, and body to create a syntax and grammar all their own. All national deaf communities don't use the same sign language! The signs from one culture to another shift and change, much like oral language changes.

Learning to observe the messages sent and received through body language is an important part of entering a new culture. Knowing the accepted way to flag down a bus or to signal agreement with a speaker, for instance, can be the difference between looking and feeling like an outsider versus living like the local members of a community.

TOUCH

Touch is a delicate element of culture because it is an intimate form of communication. There are appropriate and inappropriate ways to embrace those around you in every culture. If you mistake these you may alienate your neighbors. Deciphering when it is appropriate to hug, shake hands, or kiss is vital to understanding a people group.

The ages of those involved also play an important part in this topic. There are ways that parents may comfort their child in some parts of the world that would not be considered appropriate in other parts of the world. There are also different ideas of what is acceptable correction and discipline.

> Knowing The Languages of Culture can be the difference between looking and feeling like an outsider versus living like the local members of a community.

There is no handbook or manual that will teach you all the intricate rules of touch, but you can learn. The first step is observation. Pay special attention to how people interact with others in order to learn the nuances of touch.

SPACE

Whether it is a conscious thought or not, you have preferences and habits regarding space. How close should people sit or stand next to you? How big is an acceptable house? What is the required space for an aisle in the grocery store? As with all that has been discussed in this book, there is no universal human standard! From one group of people to another, there are different expectations of appropriate space between two people or objects. Consciously observe the distance between people in every interaction in order to understand.

TIME

Time is used in at least three important ways. Learning a culture means learning how the locals view time. First, think about how time is verbalized. Learning how people express the hour and minutes is an important piece of culture. This will also help you avoid confusion when making plans. Time standards make it possible to know when the bus will go by or when to have the kids ready for school.

Second, analyze how time is defined. An event that begins at 5:00 pm might in one culture mean the presentation starts at 5:00 on the dot. In another culture you might see people just arriving at 5:00. There are patterns and expectations about the appropriate start and end time of any event.

Finally, time is used as a point of reference. Some cultures are focused on the future and the locals will often speak in future tense. Other cultures are more likely to focus on the past, and their language will reflect that as well. There is not a universal balance between past, present, and future emphasis. Observing and recognizing the time focus of a community, however, will allow you to fit into the new culture easier.

PICTURES AND FIGURES

Illustrated symbols are another form of communication that must be observed to understand a group of people. These pictures and figures range from art that depicts elements of life to the icons that advertisers use to represent their products.

In the United States, the images on currency are widely known and respected within the nation. In Spain, the coat of arms pictured on the flag would not be naturally understood by foreigners. An international brand might have variations of their logo across the world, while a local brand's logo may be less well-known.

Every culture has symbols that mean something specific to the locals. Discerning what these pictures and figures mean and how they are important is a crucial part of observation as you are learning a new culture.

TASTE AND SMELL

Everybody knows the power of taste and smell. Every culture attaches meaning to different foods and odors. The smells and tastes of home are ingrained deeply in the hearts and minds of the people. The idea of comfort food is a reality around the world, but the actual food that brings comfort will vary widely. Learning what meal is appropriate and expected for each holiday or for comforting the sick are what you should observe in a new environment.

With smells, it is important to realize that your cultural uses may be very different from the uses of your new neighbors. What are the fragrances that are considered pleasant? Are perfumes used by people? How do they feel about room scents like incense? What odor is pleasant and what is considered unpleasant? By observing the tastes and smells of a people group, you can learn to interpret their patterns and you can use those patterns to communicate more effectively.

LIGHTS AND COLORS

Societies all over the world use colors and lights to get attention and send messages. Each culture will have different perspectives on what color is appropriate for one thing or another. What colors inspire feelings of patriotism for the country? What does red or yellow mean on a traffic sign? What colors indicate royalty? Learning to use and understand the rainbow in ways that fit the preferences and expectations of the people is yet another way to communicate effectively in a new place.

Similarly, light is just as powerful. What does a dimly lit room mean? For some it may look romantic. For others it may look suspicious, as if a crime is being planned. You might enjoy a dimly lit restaurant on a romantic date, but you would not like to go to a medical appointment where the lights are turned low!

People don't always consciously notice things like lighting and color, but they are important cultural traditions to consider. Learning to watch and seek these trends is a necessary skill for living in a new place.

SYNCING AND THE LANGUAGES OF CULTURE

Before ending this introduction to The Languages of Culture, think back to the idea of syncing. As a review, syncing is the connection of your brain waves with others due to living and acting the same. Uri Hasson, an author and researcher who has studied this level of communication, says that syncing, or coupling, relies on "shared common ground, experiences, and the beliefs people have already acquired from others."[4] Hasson is talking about syncing within a culture when people already have a shared understanding of the language and non-verbal cues. The intercultural worker wants to minimize as many distractions as possible that might hinder the free flow of thoughts. Learning to observe and correctly use The Languages of Culture reduces those distractions considerably. In fact, learning to correctly use The Languages of Culture does more than diminish distractions; it also adds to the overall communication level and to the possibility of synchronization with others.

The art of observation depends on a powerful truth. The truth is that people live according to patterns. Those patterns are called "culture" when they are shared by a large number of people and are accepted and recognized as normal.

IDENTIFYING RELATIONAL PATTERNS

Cultural patterns include the visible and obvious, like driving and walking, work hours, food, and clothing. Intercultural studies have identified other parts of life that are also patterned but less obvious.

For instance, communication patterns are cultural. Communication styles vary from one group to another, and within each group there are standards for what is acceptable. Teaching and learning is another patterned, cultural trait, leading to the popularity of intercultural education. Leadership is practiced according to the cultural patterns of a group of people and their understanding of what is appropriate. You will find intercultural leadership courses as a result of this variable.

Relationships between people is yet another area marked by distinct patterns enacted by a group of people. Just as it is important to deliberately learn the patterns of communication, education, or leadership, you should also deliberately learn the patterns of relationship when you begin to interact with new people. Interestingly, you won't find as many courses on intercultural relationships as you find for other disciplines.

> Syncing, or coupling, relies on "shared common ground, experiences, and the beliefs people have already acquired from others."

Think just a minute about the path of life that is common to all humans. You begin with a very close set of relationships. A baby will likely learn to interact with his mother first, and then slowly his group will include his father, grandparents, aunts and uncles, and older siblings. After some time the relational complexity increases and the child learns to interact with other community members like teachers, neighbors, or pastors. As he grows, his relational patterns expand so that he knows how to respond at the store or in the community.

As a person grows and develops from infancy to old age, their social and relational world changes. That complexity is not arbitrary, it is patterned. These patterns need to be understood in light of cultural expectations.

What happens to the expat who knows the appropriate way for his age group to behave in his homeland, but is unaware of what is acceptable upon moving to a different culture? How does that expat learn? How does he find a way to fit into the new expectations of cultural and social patterns?

More often than people care to admit, the adult who enters an unfamiliar culture does not deliberately learn how to interact in appropriate ways. Usually, they will only learn what is appropriate in a very narrow band of unavoidable professional and life situations. Expats are often known as those who can interact at work, the bank, stores, or salons, but who are not involved in other aspects of community life. These people never learned to see the patterns of relationship, so they feel uncomfortable in social situations and isolate themselves.

The best solution for a person experiencing unfamiliar relationship patterns is not isolation, but deliberate involvement. Just as deliberate learning can allow you to effectively understand and use The Languages of Culture, it helps you know how to behave appropriately in relationships with other people.

The following questions can help guide you as you become acquainted with the relational patterns of new people.

1. How does a person interact with a group?
    - Are all of the relationships the same?
    - What are the factors that are the same?
    - Can you describe different ways that the group and the person get along?
    - What is acceptable for all of the people involved?
    - What behavior is considered honorable or shameful?

- How should you, as a newcomer to the group, relate to the other members? You may need a coach or friend to guide you in this!
2. How does a person interact with their family?
    - What are the relational patterns between men and women who are not family?
    - What are the relational patterns between men and women who are family?
    - What are expected, normal ways for adults and children to interact? Is the expectation within family the same as expectations for children who are not in your family?
    - What is the acceptable way to interact with the elderly?
3. How does a leader interact with the people?
    - What are the patterns of interaction that you see in leaders who are highly esteemed?
    - What patterns are noticeable in the leaders who are not esteemed?
4. How should people interact socially within a large group?
    - How should people relate to one another when they are at a sporting event? A school event? A religious activity?
    - What phrases are used only in those situations? Are there special relational patterns that are unique to those contexts?
5. What are the most frequent and easy interactions?
    - Who are the people who generally do not mix or interact?
    - What are the relationships like between people who speak different languages?
    - Are there differences in relationship style depending

on the religions of the people involved? What about national or ethnic backgrounds?

You could easily create endless lists of questions to help identify the relational patterns of a group of people. These are only suggestions to help start your imagination. The big questions are, "What are the appropriate relational patterns that exist within a group of people? To what extent should an outsider adopt those relational patterns?"

> **The best solution for a person experiencing unfamiliar relationship patterns is not isolation, but deliberate involvement.**

Asking these questions will seldom lead to right/wrong answers, but rather establish what is healthy or unhealthy. It is true that there are some ways of behaving that a given people group would say are just plain wrong. More often, however, there are a range of relational patterns that are all appropriate. Some are more likely than others to foster healthy, vibrant relationships. You want to follow the patterns that will foster healthy relationships with the people in your new community. As you observe the relational patterns of the people around you, don't think in terms of right and wrong. Instead, think about what is appropriate in any given context.

There is one more idea that is relevant to relational patterns. While you observe and begin to understand the people you live among, you should always refer to the relational patterns that God says are appropriate and healthy. God's cultural patterns are the final authority. If adopting a cultural pattern requires that you go against God's commands, you should always choose to follow God. Doing so might open doors for you to explain why you choose not to participate in a specific cultural tradition.

God's values are the foundation but there are variations in how God's culture can be appropriately lived out. The Bible says, for example, to "be kind to one another, tenderhearted, forgiving one another... (Eph. 4:32)." The call is to kindness and forgiveness. The social patterns that might be appropriate for expressing that kindness and forgiveness, though, could vary widely! One culture may expect a formal conversation to recognize a moment of forgiveness. Another culture may celebrate forgiveness with a small gift and few words. Kindness and forgiveness fit God's patterns in either case, but the local cultural expressions will vary.

Relational patterns can be subtle or obvious. They can be as simple as knowing the acceptable mealtimes and forms of greeting or they can run as deep as shame/honor versus guilt/innocence. Relational patterns extend into all areas of life and culture.

To learn how to live in a new culture, learn the patterns. Learn the patterns of communication, teaching, leading, and relationship between people. Observing relational patterns in different roles and life situations is key to understanding and adapting to life in a new culture.

CHAPTER REVIEW

- What are The Languages of Culture?
- What is the ultimate goal in using The Languages of Culture?
- Why is identifying relational patterns so important when learning a new culture?

PUT IT INTO PRACTICE

- Make a list of the Languages of Culture from memory and write some examples for your own culture. Then write some that you might already know from the culture you are going to.
- How do you plan to spend time observing in an unfamiliar culture? Write down a systematic approach to your observation plans that includes the Languages of Culture.
- Review the questions that are key for understanding relational patterns. Answer these questions for your own culture. Will you be surprised to see different answers in a different culture?

CHAPTER EIGHT

Active Learning Skills

You were introduced to observation in the last few chapters, which includes many elements. There are still more skills needed for self-directed learning. In this chapter, you will discover the necessities for strengthening your knowledge of another culture and allowing your relationships with new people to thrive.

ASKING GOOD QUESTIONS

Observation is an important first step, but you will need to move forward with taking action in your relationships with new people. When you begin to converse with them, asking good questions is key to accessing the knowledge that the real experts – members of the culture who live among their own people – already have. When you go into an unfamiliar culture, you must realize that you are surrounded by people who are quite at home! They know how to use all twelve Languages of Culture.

You also need to remember that each person has their own strengths – there are poets who favor words and graphic artists who prefer to work with dimensions and colors. When you recognize these strengths, you should ask for their insight in order to better understand and work within their culture. One way to gain insight from local experts is to become skilled at asking good questions.

When thinking about asking good questions, there are some strategies that can help.
1. Avoid yes/no questions. Asking open-ended questions gives freedom to the person you are talking to. They will often answer your original question and then expound in other ways. This format will often result in unexpected glimpses into the normal patterns of the people.
2. Start with the subject that you don't understand rather than fitting your predicted answer into the question. This sounds like an obvious idea, but it is so easy to try and fit a new idea into what you already know rather than allowing it to take its own form. If you create the categories and then ask questions based on those, you force people into your choices. Asking good questions does not start with categories, but with acknowledging that you don't know something. For example, "I don't understand what I am seeing in this museum. Would you explain it?" or "I don't understand the phrase I just heard at the market. What does it mean?"

The Culture Tree can be a good tool for asking good questions. Asking people to tell the story of their town, for instance, may lead to insights that are quite different from what a history book says. Listening to their description and personal history will be helpful in understanding their patterns of life and thought. Asking how organizational patterns work in their nation will help you with practical errands and with learning how they see leadership.

The roots of The Culture Tree are where you will find asking good questions becomes more personal and difficult. When it comes to core values, beliefs, and expectations, it is not uncommon for people to feel hesitant in their answers. Questions about the roots may be better answered by finding the poets, filmmakers, writers, and leaders who have embodied those values and truths. When you ask for a book or singer who represents the heart of the people, you may find more success than simply asking someone about their core beliefs and values.

PAYING ATTENTION

Among the tools that serve well for learning the lifestyle of a new culture, the ability to pay attention is perhaps the most powerful. This doesn't mean simply noticing the words, colors, or physical proximity that people might share. Those elements are easy to notice and comprehend without much thought. Paying attention refers to full mental focus on the conversations around you – an active learning with empathy and sympathy. This level of attention demands new skills for most people.

Think about a typical day for the average person. Steve wakes up fairly early and almost immediately reviews his schedule. He dresses according to the events on his calendar. He thinks about the emotions he has toward his upcoming day.

Over breakfast he talks with his wife about his schedule for that day. After he goes to the office, he reads the messages for five different email accounts and the notifications for two social media sites.

All of his thinking is aimed "out there." He is focused on getting the job done, whatever that job might be.

How about your day? It might be pretty similar. Perhaps there is a radio show or podcast in the mix if you have a long enough commute. Perhaps there is a time to read a book or pack lunches for the family before everyone heads out the door. The point is that most people focus an overwhelming amount of energy on engaging with forces, situations, and beings outside of themselves. They are so busy "doing" that they don't have time to "be."

This life pattern has its own pros and cons. Counselors and pastors can guide that conversation, but when it comes to intercultural engagement, you have to develop a new pattern. You have to learn to move from just doing to reflecting, thinking, asking, and learning. You need a way to force yourself to pay attention to the patterns around you. You have to develop the skill of slowing your mind down enough so you can learn patterns instead of simply pursuing actions.

> **Paying attention refers to full mental focus on the conversations around you. It's an active learning with empathy and sympathy.**

There are five skills that will help you to become an intentional listener and truly engaged with those you are speaking to. When these become second nature, you will find it hard to be a passive learner.

SKILL #1: WTGA

Looking at almost any cultural adaptation course, you will find some version of a learning cycle. WTGA is the way CultureBound approaches this idea. WTGA stands for Watch, Think, Guess, Act/Ask.

The first step is to watch. This refers back to the discussion on observation. Pay attention to The Languages of Culture. The situation here has nothing to do with "why" an event took place, it is simply descriptive. What happened? How did that occur? Who was present? What were the actions?

Pretend you are thirsty and want to buy a soft drink. You are in an open-air market, and don't know exactly what to do. You see someone walk by holding a bottle that looks like what you have in mind. You then look for the vendor who sells that drink. Soon you find him in his stand. Now you are not sure how to buy the drink, so you watch other people. How do they purchase the soft drink? Do they form a queue? Do they ask for the product by name? You watch those who know what to do.

The next step is to think or reflect. You still are not asking "why" but you definitely want to think below the surface about what happened. This part of the learning cycle allows you to rehearse in your mind what took place and what you observed. Think about the starting points of the action and the results that grew from the action.

In the soft drink example, you are going to move from observing how other people get their soft drinks to thinking about how you can get one. Thinking about what you have seen, you acknowledge that you will need to get the drink and pay for it. You have watched the pattern and you have thought about the way that you might fit into that pattern. It is important to note that most situations are not as straightforward as buying a soft drink in an open-air market! Other situations will need a lot more thought.

> When it comes to paying attention in everyday situations, one of the key skills is learning to deliberately watch, think, guess, and act.

It is now time to guess the appropriate action to take. It is now appropriate to ask how to be involved. It is helpful to think about what might have happened if this action had been different.

Guessing about the desired outcomes and options behind the action will give you confidence to perform the action yourself.

In the soft drink situation, what if you had noticed that only young children were buying the drinks, but you are in your mid-twenties? You might guess then that what you are viewing is how children order and you need to further observe adults. On the other hand, you could guess that even though mostly children are ordering, it makes sense that adults would order the same way. In either case, you are making an educated guess of the patterns of the people. You have watched and thought about things, so you use that analysis to guess the most likely way that you should act.

You are ready to get feedback via acting or asking. It is time to act on your guess and see the response of those around you. You can gauge positive or negative feedback based on the response to your actions or words. In either case, you want to act in the way that seems most appropriate. When you do that, carefully watch the people around you to observe their reaction. You might see the reaction in their eyes or hear it in their words, but their response is key for learning.

You guessed that even though you only see children ordering, it would be appropriate for you as well. You follow what you have seen them do by getting a soft drink from the fridge and taking it to the cashier. In a positive feedback situation, he might nod or smile, take your payment, and thank you for your patronage. In a negative feedback situation, he might look confused or upset and then tell you that drinks in the fridge are only for children. He might then instruct you how to get a drink.

Both outcomes are ultimately positive for you as a learner. It may be uncomfortable to receive negative feedback, but it allows you to understand the actions of the culture. In some instances, the uncomfortability of being corrected is more impactful because you will be sure to correct yourself in order to avoid future discomfort.

When it comes to paying attention in everyday situations, one of the key skills is learning to deliberately watch, think, guess, and act. As you repeat that process and receive feedback, you will develop insight into the cultural patterns of the people you are among while also becoming a skilled learner.

SKILL #2: INTENTIONALITY

When it comes to paying attention to the situations and people around you, one of the most powerful skills is intentionality. Knowing what you need to learn and purposely striving to learn it will lead to many bridges of understanding.

The normal pattern for most people, however, is to focus so much on buying groceries or picking up the mail that they do not intentionally register the conversation with the clerk or the work patterns of those who are sorting mail. To be intentional is not to neglect the groceries or mail, rather to go about daily activities with heightened mindfulness in order to learn what is appropriate in the situation. It is not entirely different from what you normally do. It is adding to the normal life patterns you already have in order to become a deliberate learner.

Books on sociological themes call this "participant observation." It is the process of going about the actions of life, while at the same time being intentional in noticing the specific results, reactions, and influences of your actions. Intentionality is required for living and learning a new culture.

SKILL #3: SYMPATHY

If you are to live in a new culture, you must sympathize with the people of that culture. The English dictionary has two distinct definitions for sympathy. The first is a feeling of sorrow or pity for someone in difficulty. While this is important to keep in mind, you can focus on the second definition. Sympathy is an understanding between people or a common feeling between two or more people.

When you enter a new culture, developing a sense of what you already have in common with the people is a strong tool for adjustment. This starts with acknowledging humanity and leads to recognition that there are many possible ways to meet the needs that all people face. Those distinct patterns vary across cultures, but at their root they point to the humanity that connects all people. That recognition of what is in common and what is different ranges from the superficial, like forks versus chopsticks, to the deeply significant, like correcting wrong behaviors through shame versus guilt. In any case, you can develop sympathy with anyone you come in contact with.

Though the differences are real and deep, at the core all people face very similar difficulties. The one path for salvation through Jesus Christ is a clear recognition by God that in spite of the differences between generations, ethnicities, and cultures, there is a common human situation. Learning to recognize commonalities among your new neighbors is pivotal in learning how to fully pay attention for cultural development.

SKILL #4: EMPATHY

A closely related skill for the intercultural worker is empathy, which is the ability to personalize the feelings and responses of another person. While sympathy is important for the learner, empathy is perhaps even more crucial. You start with sympathy and recognize the commonality that exists between people. You graduate to empathy in order to understand the other person's response to their circumstances. Empathy is the ability to imagine that you are living the reality of the other person, allowing you to understand the how and why behind a person's actions.

Sympathy develops a recognition of similarities, while empathy develops the perspective of how a person responds to those similarities. It is not possible to empathize in a passive way. It is an active skill.

SKILL #5: BUILDING BRIDGES

In order to pay full attention, you must draw conclusions and make connections. Building bridges between yourself and a new person is an active process. As you grow in understanding the realities of life in another culture, you will also realize that developing relationships is possible but not automatic. You will realize that a bridge has to be built. Building relationships is a deliberate process that requires recognizing the experiences of both sets of people and finding ways to interact that considers both experiences.

This idea of building bridges could look like many things. It could be one person choosing to welcome immigrants by acknowledging they probably feel uncomfortable in the neighborhood. The person might offer to teach them the life patterns of their new community. It could look like language lessons or cooking classes. It could look like a shared celebration of a national holiday.

For those whose intercultural experience involves moving to another land, building a bridge could include the willingness to be a learner as well as a teacher. For many people, being a willing learner is harder than being a willing teacher. Humility, graciousness, and patience are required when learning from others.

Building bridges is not a skill that allows for apathy. You must pay close attention, be an active listener, and engage with many people in order to accomplish the ultimate goal of establishing relationships and learning a new culture.

GETTING INVOLVED

Learning to live and work in a culture different than your own includes a lot of trial and error. The WTGA cycle highlights this point. Dr. Donald Smith says, "Communication is involvement." [5]

Involvement is not as easy as it sounds, but fortunately it isn't terribly difficult either. Getting involved requires flexibility and a willingness to try. It is being open to trying new foods, activities, and daily life patterns. These will all be different from what you are used to. Being involved means using the transportation system that your neighbors use, even if you prefer a different way. Involvement requires that you seek out and expect change to your default way of living.

> The one path for salvation through Jesus Christ is a clear recognition by God that in spite of the differences between generations, ethnicities, and cultures, there is a common human situation.

There are limits, of course, and each person must recognize them. It is one thing to eat new foods, but a medical condition might limit your ability to be involved. Public ceremonies are good events to attend, but what if they involve worship or recognition of spirits that are contrary to God? Involvement is a skill that includes discernment. The ultimate goal is to build relationships and open lines of communication. Staying involved while also staying true to your beliefs is a balancing act necessary for cultural immersion.

TAKING NOTES

You have read several times that culture is the study of patterns.

As people develop their ways of thinking, talking, feeling, and behaving, consistent patterns form. The intentional search for the patterns of a group of people is really the key to learning a new culture.

In this search for patterns, you will use the powerful tool of observation. There is an additional tool that is needed with observation. In order to remember what you observe, you must record. Your mind is not as good at memorizing as you might think. People are best at remembering what affects them emotionally, so they focus less on the details of life as it flows by.

When you enter into a new culture, this often means that you will mostly recall situations that were uncomfortable. When you have heard expats talking about their host culture, isn't this exactly the topic of conversation? They frequently share moments that were difficult, embarrassing, sad, threatening, or that didn't make sense.

There is a simple remedy for this lack of ability to remember the patterns of another group of people. The solution is taking notes. This tool is often neglected, but it can be immensely helpful when observing a new culture. As you are observing, or shortly after, jot down the who, what, why, where, when, and how of a situation and review your notes frequently.

Be careful to only write notes about what you have actually seen, heard, tasted, or in some other way experienced! The temptation is to write notes about your interpretations, like the way you felt or what you imagined was the reason for some word or action. If you can resist that temptation and instead only write down the actual words, sounds, time of day, or flavors, then you will start to see patterns develop.

Why are notes so powerful? In the moment of observation, patterns might not be obvious. When you record over time and review your notes, you will better be able to make the mental connections that you didn't see before. You won't always remember the common actions you observe, but you can identify trends in your notes from many different experiences.

The good news is that taking notes has never been easier! In the digital age, you always have the ability to take notes on your phone. You could also carry a notebook and write if you prefer. You might find digital note taking more convenient because of the search function. There are pros and cons for both approaches.

Don't be concerned about formatting or display. These notes are not for public consumption! The only audience is you, and the main purpose is for you to recall what you saw in the moment. A helpful tip is to always note the place and time of an observation. Patterns, after all, are tied to times of day, days of the week, and certain places. Including those details will help patterns to appear more quickly.

In the next chapter you will read about the value of habits. Taking notes regularly is a habit you should adopt in order to aid your learning efforts in a new culture.

FOLLOWING EXPERTS

Over the course of this chapter, the focus has been on self-directed learning. You have read the importance of observing, asking, and paying attention. At this point you might be wondering why it has not been suggested that you read books or resources by anthropologists or other cultural experts.

While cultural experts can offer some great help, their help is limited. It is difficult to become an "expert" of a different culture because any group of people will have a wide range of diversity. A book written about a group of people will be limited to generalizations that may or may not be true in the exact community where you live. Since issues like local history and geography affect lifestyle, you have to expect that what is written for a large group of people located across a vast area will only partially reflect the realities of any specific subgroup.

Additionally, cultures grow, develop, and change! What is written this year may not be accurate next year and will almost certainly be modified over the course of 25 or 30 years.

Even though these limitations exist, experts do have value. You should research what social scientists, historians, and anthropologists have to say about your own culture and the culture you are going to. The key is to read that information AFTER you have done your own study. Your insights are best when they grow directly from the local community and what patterns you see.

After you have started to recognize those patterns, you can read the experts with your own perspective in mind. You will undoubtedly learn new facts and gain new insights. Those are valuable! It's important to not let the generalities made in research replace your local insights. If you learn directly first, then anything learned from experts can be filtered through the lens of your experience in the local community.

CONSUMING MEDIA

Another source for learning about a new culture is their own art, books, music, shows, and other media. How do they tell their story? Music and art can be powerful mediums for expression. Consuming media is a surefire way to learn the appropriate patterns of other people. You could get more insight from one song than from a 300-page book by someone who is not a local. Listening to artists and paying attention to the words, concepts, and values that they express will give you a glimpse into their heart and mind.

ESTABLISHING HABITS

In his recent book called The Power of Habit, author and researcher Charles Duhigg talks about how humans create habits for some 40% or more of their daily activities.[22] These habits are culturally informed! This leads to two striking applications.

First, you should learn the habits of your neighbors, and make them your own habits to the level that you can. Learning the patterns of a new culture can also be understood as learning the habits that are shared by a group of people. Those patterns or habits all relate to the human condition and they all can be learned as you enter a new culture. Duhigg writes about the process of learning a new habit by focusing on the cues, performance, and rewards of that habit. As you go about learning a new habit, it turns out that new cues and rewards are key, much more than simply deciding to do things differently. To a great degree, learning to live and work in an unfamiliar culture is the process of developing new habits that better sync with the patterns of the people.

> God's faithfulness added to your effort equals quality and meaningful relationships with those from a different culture.

A goal of this book is to push you to develop the habit of being a self-directed learner. It can start with simple things like putting your notebook with The Languages of Culture in your coat pocket every night so that every morning you see a cue to observe. Give yourself both social and physical rewards. The joy of new discoveries is pretty addicting. There is nothing quite as satisfying as having someone say, "You understand us." When you are a self-directed learner, it is easier for you to grow deeper in your relationships with the people around you.

There is another sense in which habits are of critical importance. Duhigg explains that some habits are "keystone habits." These habits are foundational because when you have a keystone habit, it is more natural to keep other smaller habits. As an example, writing and reviewing written notes that record the who, what, when, where, and how of your observations is a keystone habit. With that habit you will find yourself developing a plan for writing notes. You will develop a tool for remembering The Languages of Culture. You will find yourself wondering and thinking about how to ask questions to better understand a situation. Much of what is discussed in this chapter will coalesce into new habits of thought and action simply because you are being intentional about writing your observations.

BE AN ACTIVE LEARNER

In summary, the skills for being self-directed in culture learning include observing, identifying patterns, asking good questions, paying attention, getting involved, taking notes, following experts, consuming media, and establishing habits. In the experience of expats who have spent many years living and working in different cultures, these processes have made it possible for them to progress in understanding and being understood. No one can teach you about the culture you are going to, but you can learn by becoming disciplined in these areas. God's faithfulness added to your effort equals quality and meaningful relationships with those from a different culture. These relationships open the door for you to participate in the mission of every tribe, language, people, and nation.

CHAPTER REVIEW

- What are the skills for self-directed learning?
- What are some examples of self-directed learning?
- What is a keystone habit?

PUT IT INTO PRACTICE

- Make a list of the skills for self-directed learning and come up with a scenario for how you can use each skill.
- Buy or find a notebook and decorate or add photos to the cover. Use this notebook to take notes on your observations in a new culture.
- Do some research into the "experts" of the culture you are going to. Compile a list of music, artwork, and books you can consume in order to connect with the people.

CHAPTER NINE

Active Learning Attitudes

✤

Like so much of life, learning to live and work in an unfamiliar culture is a beautiful mixture of outward insights and skills and inward attitudes. You have read about the outward-focused habits like observation, asking good questions, consulting with experts, and taking notes. In this chapter, you will learn the inner attitudes that help you move toward better cultural adaptation and adjustment.

MILTON BENNETT'S SIX STAGES OF INTERCULTURAL SENSITIVITY

Intercultural trainer Milton J. Bennett developed a six-stage model for describing a person's orientation with respect to a culture. The Developmental Model of Intercultural Sensitivity (DMIS) describes a perspective from highly ethnocentric to highly ethnorelative. The six stages of the DMIS model show the human attitude as it progresses in relation to another culture.[23]

You will read about the six stages in the coming pages, but it is most important to recognize the two major divisions at the root of the DMIS model. The ethnocentric view addresses other cultures with the mindset of, "My ways are best." The ethnorelative view approaches differences in cultures with the mindset of, "All ways can be good."

As with so much of the intercultural world, there is a great truth in ethnorelativism and yet it can also be misleading.

The great truth is that your way of living is not necessarily any better or worse than the lifestyle of someone from another culture. People naturally compare new situations with what they have previously experienced. That is normal and usually serves you well within your own cultural patterns. The danger comes when you compare cultures on the basis of right and wrong. Your ways are not automatically right and their ways are not automatically wrong. There are many times when you will need to learn to recognize that things are different, not necessarily right or wrong.

Think, for example, about how people in different cultures eat, how they address good manners, or how their workers and bosses might interact. In those situations, there is great wisdom when you learn to think of their intuitive patterns as different, not wrong. The concept of ethnorelative thinking, however, has limits.

> **Learning to live and work in an unfamiliar culture is a beautiful mixture of outward insights and skills and inward attitudes.**

The misleading part of this is that there is a standard that is not relative, but is firm and stable. This standard is the Word of God. It is the foundation of comparison for all cultures and all people. The really powerful part of this truth is that your home culture has just as much change required as the new culture you are entering when compared with God's word.

In horizontal terms, the DMIS model is of great value. In terms of God's word, however, you will see an absolute moral standard rather than just recognizing what is a different life pattern.

STAGE ONE: DENIAL

In order to stay in their emotional and cognitive comfort zone, people begin by denying that there are any differences between cultures. This stage is seen as a way to maintain stability in the presence of increased diversity.

It might be easy to focus solely on your experiences when comparing cultures. As noted throughout this book, being aware of common human struggles is in fact a pathway to improved empathy and better intercultural work. This awareness, however, does not deny intercultural differences. After you acknowledge the similarities, you also need to identify the differences within the context of human experiences.

STAGE TWO: DEFENSE

The next attitude toward people of a different culture is defensiveness of your own patterns and ways of life. Often these defenses come with criticisms of the new patterns of life. "My way is best" implies that other ways are inferior or even wrong.

If you want to grow out of that defensive posture, you have to learn to see many possible ways of life. You must learn to replace the stereotypes of "how they do things" with a more nuanced perspective that there are many ways to deal with the issues of life. The best options will differ from one cultural context to another. Not everything about life is relative, but there are many ways to live a God-honoring life. Defending the normal approaches of your own culture is not usually necessary or helpful.

STAGE THREE: MINIMIZATION

A third stage in Bennett's model is more ethnorelative than

denial or defensiveness. The minimization stage is when a person acknowledges differences but considers them unimportant. In this stage, the attitude is that you share underlying values, specifically the values from your own culture. Instead of seeing differences for what they are, this perspective minimizes the differences to ultimately being the same deep down.

As with all these attitudes, it is important to identify the key error in this pattern that Bennett calls "minimization." That error is thinking that everyone shares the same basic values. Humans really differ in principles, and recognizing those differences is not only honest, but is required for healthy relationships.

Minimization is all about trying to find common values to explain behaviors divergent from what you expect. The CultureBound model sees humanity as united in the human condition. This doesn't necessarily mean you have the same values. You should work to form relationships that cross the differences between cultures.

Minimization is the last stage before the shift from ethnocentrism (focusing on your own culture) to ethnorelativism (accepting many cultures).

STAGE FOUR: ACCEPTANCE

Eventually, you will see that other cultures are also complex and intricate. This is called acceptance. When you accept their complexity, you can describe cultures in terms that are accurate from their perspective.

Acceptance does not compare opinions against an authoritative standard. There is not a sense of right and wrong at this level. It is simply a recognition and agreement that every culture is different in many ways. As a Christian educator or communicator, there is a standard of right and wrong, so this attitude of acceptance should be balanced. You are accepting people from other cultures as they are, not necessarily accepting their beliefs as truth. From a human point of view, people live in a wide variety of ways that must be accepted. In terms of Christian communication, all cultural traditions should be compared and evaluated in light of Scripture.

STAGE FIVE: ADAPTATION

In the fifth stage of the DMIS, a person is able to see life through the eyes of another person and another culture. It is deeper than simple acceptance; this level of intercultural involvement allows you to adapt to their perspective.

One of the difficulties with people who have adapted is that they may be comfortable enough to shift across many different cultures. They may start to lose their identity in this case. They can put themselves into the position of so many other people that they may struggle to remember their core.

Even if this is not a difficulty, it is often a concern or criticism of friends and family. The well-adapted intercultural worker will have a small but firm self-identity while also having a deep flexibility to grasp and respond to life circumstances of people from other cultures.

STAGE SIX: INTEGRATION

Bennett's sixth stage can be understood in both organizational and personal levels as an augmented ability to think and act in ways that fit a new culture. This person has created a third culture – it is not their home culture or the culture where they live, but a hybrid. They are able to have dynamic interaction with others who have also grown in that nexus of cultural patterns.

The church is theoretically a perfect place for integration. The point is not to develop "my patterns" or "your patterns," but to create a third culture that shows God's kingdom values in practical outworking among people from a given community.

ATTITUDES

When looking at the six attitudes and perspectives in the DMIS model, you can start to identify attitudes that are healthy and unhealthy.

It is unhealthy to form judgments that consider one culture to be superior to another culture. Also, blind acceptance that all cultures are appropriate and equally good is a dangerous attitude to have. A naïve belief that everyone is the same or that everyone has the same core values and beliefs is detrimental to learning.

> **An attitude of adjustment in cultural practices that is matched with a firm understanding of your own roots is the idea behind flexibility.**

It is healthy to understand what each culture really believes, values, and considers appropriate. You need a level of humility that recognizes good and bad as God defines them, not based on the practice of any given culture. It is positive to have a level of empathy that puts you in the shoes of a person from another culture. A healthy attitude includes willingness and ability to integrate diverse cultures into the new creation that is the church. Think about the healthy attitudes that are required as a culture learner.

FLEXIBILITY

This book is directed towards people who either now or soon will live and work within the context of another culture. Perhaps you are reading it as one who will be traveling to live as an expat in another land. Perhaps your ministry is geared toward migrants arriving in your homeland. You may not be going to their part of the world, but you are getting close enough to help them adjust to life in your homeland. In either case, a flexible mindset is of utmost importance in ministry.

A gym trainer might say that if you want to be truly strong, you need to work on stretching in addition to weights. You need both flexibility and strength. This is a close analogy for intercultural interactions. To be flexible, you have to be strong. To be strong, it is important to be flexible.

An author in the area of cultural intelligence, Julia Middleton, uses the words "core" and "flex" to talk about these two related concepts.[24]

The best intercultural workers have a core that is strong in terms of self-awareness and recognition. The person with a strong core knows their own non-negotiable values, beliefs, and priorities. Interestingly, this strong self-awareness is considered by Middleton to be the best indicator of an aptitude for intercultural life and work.

Paired with this core foundation is the idea of flex. The strong core is matched with an equal willingness to be flexible in many other ways. In light of The Culture Tree, a strong core refers to solid roots. Flex includes virtually everything else. All of the above-ground elements require various levels of flexibility, including interaction with the physical environment, adaptability to different government forms, differences in personal interaction, and a willingness to share unfamiliar work habits. All of these above-ground issues might vary from one culture to another. An attitude of adjustment in cultural practices that is matched with a firm understanding of your own roots is the idea behind flexibility.

The apostle Paul is an example of core and flex. He knew the gospel and built his core around that, however, to the Jews he was a Jew, and to the Greeks a Greek (1 Cor. 9:19-23). Throughout the

New Testament you see Paul's flexibility with his travel, his food, and his companions. He would preach the word in season and out of season. Even when he was incarcerated, he kept his spirit open to use the opportunities available for his core calling to proclaim the Gospel. His foundation was solid and defined, and he adapted in just about everything else.

People are not all as flexible as Paul, but it is worth developing awareness of your own core. A personal statement of the values and truths that you cannot and will not change is a strong tool for all kinds of ministry. At the same time, learning to be flexible about how you live life is necessary for intercultural relationships.

WITHHOLDING JUDGMENT

Humility in many different forms is another attitude that is necessary for intercultural ministry. One great illustration of humility is the ability to withhold judgment. In many educational situations, teachers push people to make a decision or to express their opinion about different issues. That can be a good strategy in a classroom situation. In real life, however, the humility to wait until all of the facts have been gathered and the right questions have been asked is even more valuable.

Your first impression might serve you well in your home culture. When you are learning a set of core beliefs, values, and relationship patterns new to you, there is a lot of possibility for error when you jump to conclusions.

If you have lived and worked with people from a different culture, think about the times when you misinterpreted their words, facial expressions, or motives. If you have not had that experience, ask someone who has lived overseas for any period of time. If that person got involved with the community around them, they will definitely have stories of times when they initially misunderstood some part of the culture. They will also tell you that with time they grew to appreciate those parts of the culture in new ways.

Maybe it was a facial expression that was originally misunderstood. Perhaps it was the way that a meeting was run that left someone disillusioned. Perhaps a meal that just didn't seem appropriate was served. In any of those or a thousand other scenarios, the person involved would have done well to withhold judgment.

You should not eliminate judgment, rather postpone, withhold, pause, or slow down. When there has been time to fully grasp the situation and the nuances involved, then you can interpret the meaning of what has been experienced. Before that clarity is available, it is an essential and vital skill to withhold judgment.

> **Develop your opinion when you must and learn to patiently wait before that.**

There was a man who worked with a group that provides testing services for intercultural situations. His first experience with the group was very uncomfortable. Feeling rejected, he steered clear of that group for a couple of years until he had an unavoidable need to reconnect. The second time, he did some deeper research before his involvement and learned several facts that he didn't know before. Those newly understood facts changed the entire scenario. He could look at the situations from that first encounter and appreciate how they had responded. His only regret, as you can probably imagine, was that he didn't deliberately withhold judgment in the first place before learning more about them. Withholding judgment would have saved him unnecessary emotional ups and downs, and even more importantly it would have established a healthy relationship earlier.

The lesson? An attitude of humility will serve you well in intercultural situations where you probably don't understand all of the elements that you see at play. In these situations, it is best to delay your opinions. Withhold judgement until you are quite sure that all of the facts are clear and everyone has had a chance to explain and speak to the situation. After you have fully understood, you might find that your original opinion is the same, or you might find that you have changed your mind. In either case, don't disregard the final opinion. You need to identify how you feel about the topic, and you may need to report and support your opinion. Forming your opinion slowly will help you withhold unnecessary negative judgement. Develop your opinion when you must and learn to patiently wait before that.

SELF-DIRECTION

For those taught in a formal school setting, one of the bad habits that is often developed is a passive approach to learning. For some people, the teacher simply knows best and so they naturally follow the guidance and instruction of the teacher. For others, perhaps it never crossed their mind that they should or could take an active role in learning! Outside of memorizing the facts, figures, and flow of thought received from a teacher, their job as learners was to accept the teacher's statements in an unassertive manner.

That attitude does not work well for most of life, and it really doesn't help when it comes to learning how to live and work in an unfamiliar culture. In the culture learning arena, you have to be self-motivated and self-directed. Culture learning requires that the learner take responsibility for their own progress.

Look at this self-directed learning idea from two levels: understanding the elements needed for self-directed learning and making self-directed learning into a habit.

Since Malcolm Knowles popularized the idea of self-directed

learning in the 1970s, there have been some key concepts associated with the idea.[25]

1. Identify the specific skills, knowledge, or attitudes that the learner needs (needs assessment).
2. Prepare the learner with activities or discussions (learning readiness).
3. Identify the goals for learning.
4. Create and use a learning plan.
5. Evaluate the results.

These five steps are typically considered part of the working relationship between a teacher and an adult learner. Learning contracts are created where a facilitator with previous experience and subject knowledge will provide some level of structure while the learner brings motivation, curiosity, and desire for growth in the process.

In a culture-learning situation, however, this level of self-directed learning is not usually feasible because the learner probably does not have just one teacher who is providing that subject-matter expertise. In a culture-learning situation, the learner has to take an even more active role. They need to define what they want to learn in terms that are as specific as possible, estimate their readiness to learn that information, set out the specific process by which they plan to learn, use that plan, and then evaluate to see if the goals were met.

As an example, consider an American who moves to Brazil and wants to learn to drive in his new city of Recife. The new driver in this cultural activity is Ted. What would it look like for Ted to be self-directed as a learner through the 5 learning concepts?

1. For a needs assessment, Ted might say that he needs to be able to get to his company office that is about 30 minutes away, and using public transport is not a good option for him.
2. To establish learning readiness, Ted might realize that he is

not yet ready to navigate traffic because he needs to learn other things first, like the formal rules of driving and how to read the Portuguese road signs.
3. Ted has identified starting goals, so he learns a bit of Portuguese and he finds the formal rules of the road. He lists other goals like searching for driving schools, asking colleagues in his new office for some suggestions, and learning the legal requirements for him as an expat.
4. Ted is ready to create and start his learning plan. He will learn to drive the way that the driving school or his office colleagues suggest. He takes the necessary steps to follow through with these required actions.
5. When Ted has completed driving school, he will evaluate to see if he is driving in a way that seems to fit the flow of traffic. He sets a goal of mastering driving in 3 months, and wants to be as natural as possible in his new city. He decides that the level of natural driving for Recife is marked by other drivers treating him like they treat everyone else. His first lesson is to observe how other drivers treat one another. How often are horns used? Are there hand gestures that people use when they are driving? What do those gestures mean? What kinds of traffic patterns indicate the flow of traffic? What traffic patterns are recognized by gestures, honks, or yelling? Can those patterns be identified?

Being self-directed as a learner is a matter of attitude as well as skill. There are perhaps three attitudes that best summarize this kind of self-directed learning.
- You must take responsibility for your own growth
- You need perseverance in continuing to apply this process to one topic after another over the years. Every time there is a new life circumstance, the cycle repeats! After Ted

learns to drive, he will need to know how to behave at a funeral, how to interact appropriately in vacation spots, how to interact with the doctor in an office visit, and so much more. That persistence for learning each scenario is a core part of self-directed culture learning.
- You need a creative mindset to consider the best way to learn what you don't know. Where can you go to learn how to drive? How do you learn to buy groceries? Where will you take university courses? Being creative is a big part of knowing how to be a self-directed learner.

> The courage to make mistakes, the resilience to learn from them, and the ability to move past them are all major strengths in self-directed learners.

Stanislas Dehaene is a more recent author who ties learning together with advances in neuroscience.[9] He lists four pillars of learning which also touch on attitudes. According to Dehaene, the four pillars of learning are:
1. Focused attention
2. Active engagement
3. Error feedback
4. Daily rehearsal with nightly consolidation

There are, once again, repeated attitudes inherent in these four pillars.

Focused attention reminds you that learning is work. It can be pleasant and interesting, but it is not a passive event that just happens to you. The person who needs to learn how to live and work in an unfamiliar culture does well to develop that mental toughness.

Active engagement is the choice to attend to the situation instead of letting the opportunity pass you by. Someone who is actively engaged will also be creative at finding the people, places, and situations that best facilitate learning.

Error feedback can be especially challenging, and will especially reflect attitude. This is the idea that when you make errors, you need to accept those as learning opportunities and not as defeats. It has been said that it takes courage to learn a culture. You will make mistakes and you will have to see those mistakes in a positive light. The alternative to that courageous attitude is self-defense. This attitude is common and self-sabotaging. The only way to learn cultural involvement is to be engaged with what you don't yet fully understand! Mistakes are part of the process, and learning from errors is much more effective than trying to learn from successes. The courage to make mistakes, the resilience to learn from them, and the ability to move past them are all major strengths in self-directed learners.

Finally, daily rehearsal with nightly consolidation are key pillars of learning. The attitude of persistence is, once again, visible here. Ted will have to practice driving daily in order to learn. He will then have to practice language and review. He will have to practice interacting with others. Self-directed learning is not a "one-and-done" skill. It is fine to take a break for a bit, but the successful culture learner will keep going day after day for the long haul.

Repeating the following statements will help you to evaluate and commit yourself to self-directed learning.
- I take responsibility for learning how to live and work in an unfamiliar culture.
- I have persevered in learning before and I will now keep learning any given cultural situation until I am able to

complete it as part of my normal, daily flow of life.
- I will persevere in learning one new situation after another for as long as I need to. Each new life circumstance will take me into new learning circumstances and I will keep going.
- I will identify what I want and need to learn, and I will put creative energy into figuring out how I can learn those topics.
- I recognize that learning is not a passive activity, but an active one. I will act accordingly!
- I will evaluate my actions fairly, and I will recognize when I get it right. Even more importantly, I will recognize when I get it wrong, and in those moments I will choose the courageous path of honesty and accepting the error as a powerful learning opportunity.
- I accept that God himself is part of the learning process. When I lack wisdom, I can call on him. He teaches in many different ways. Occasionally, he gives me supernatural direction for how things should be done. He works to help me be persistent and courageous to learn through natural processes. He can providentially bring people into my path who can teach me what I need to know, and he can put me into learning situations today that will prepare me for larger challenges tomorrow.

FORMING HABITS

Self-directed learning is the foundation for cultural adaptation and adjustment. The successful intercultural worker will strive to make learning a habit. As author Charles Duhigg points out, nearly half of a person's daily actions grow from decisions made long ago.[22] They are habits of thought, behavior, and response. You don't recreate every new situation, but instead you create habits that guide you through both new and old situations.

In culture learning, the problem is that the habits from your homeland are probably completely inappropriate in a new context! You cannot trust those habits to be acceptable and appropriate in a new area. You can, however, dedicate yourself to creating a habit of learning.

Habits, it turns out, are based on three keys: a cue, a response, and a reward.

When you enter cultural situations that are unfamiliar, you will be reminded to learn if you create a cue. This could be as simple as recognizing you don't understand something and immediately trying to figure it out. That is your cue to actively learn.

You then create the response mechanism. This is the action step. You identify your need for learning by your cues and you set out to learn through a variety of methods that were discussed previously.

Finally, you can create rewards in order to solidify the learning habit in your brain.

There is one set of rewards that is inherent to human learning, and that is the hormonal response of dopamine release. When you succeed in accomplishing a self-directed goal, your brain rewards you with happy-feeling chemicals. That jolt of pleasure is a strong reward! This is similar to the feeling you get when you synchronize with others and reach a deeper level of communication.

Culture learning can deliberately include other rewards too. You are rewarded when you review your notes and see how far you've come. Writing, blogging, or creating a video presentation of what you've learned could be another reward. When you experience true learning, you are motivated to share your progress with others.

You can also reward yourself for accomplishing a task. Make goals and then treat yourself with a dinner out or a trip to the park when that goal is met. You can also work with other people who give social feedback rewards for progress.

Perhaps the most direct reward is the ability to perform the new thing you've learned. Learning to drive or learning the language can be huge steps toward building relationships with the locals. Culture learning tends to open doors in the life of the community in very exciting ways. When you make self-directed learning a habit, you are set up for building successful relationships in a new culture.

SELF-DISCIPLINE

While you are developing the habit of learning, you will need the attitude of self-discipline. This will help you to cultivate the keystone habits of a culture learner. Keystone habits, as mentioned before, are fairly simple habits that open the door for many other good habits to follow.

What are some of the keystone habits of culture learning?
- Observing
- Taking notes
- Reviewing notes
- Asking good questions
- Consulting experts
- Withholding judgment

The self-discipline it takes to form each of those activities into a habit will make all the difference for the person who lives in an unfamiliar context! Those small habits, persistently applied, will allow for learning how to live, minister, talk, converse, cook, drive, work, and so much more. Thousands of habits that you need to develop to be comfortable in a new culture are unleashed by developing those basic keystone habits. Once you develop the keystone habits, the door is open for a lifetime of ongoing learning. This doesn't happen overnight and requires a high level of self-discipline in order to be successful.

COMMUNITY

When entering an unfamiliar culture, it is important to have the mindset of working with others rather than solely focusing on individuality. While there are many reasons for individual initiative and responsibility in the culture learning process, culture is by definition the way that a group of people interact. You cannot be a solitary, isolated person and also be successful in cultural integration. The much better alternative is to pursue culture learning in a community.

> **When you succeed in accomplishing a self-directed goal, your brain rewards you with happy-feeling chemicals.**

Perhaps you have moved into a new culture with family or with others from your homeland. That group of people can be an asset for culture learning or a detriment. Think about what happens when the learning community is made of expats versus those who come from within the unfamiliar culture.

The expat group can serve to strengthen and help the culture learner when several people decide to walk through the process together. You can take the weight of learning a new culture off your shoulders by working with others to share new insights, create a shared document with observations, think and pray together about how to interact effectively, recommend resources, and so much more. There are many healthy ways that people working in a community can encourage and help each other so that all grow in their culture learning together.

This group can also be detrimental. Sometimes it's easy to pick up negative attitudes like criticism and condemnation. A small group that gathers at the end of the day to laugh at their new neighbors, criticize their bad manners, or judge the way that people live does much more harm than good. Instead of helping each other grow in effective outreach, these toxic attitudes will lead to judgmental and dismissive behaviors. If you find your group becoming negative toward the culture you are supposed to serve, it is time to seek a serious attitude adjustment and deliberate behavior changes so that those negative roots do not grow any deeper.

There is another way that a community can turn negative. While it is great for a group to decide to learn together, it can be disastrous when one or two people take on the role of the teacher, while others act as students. The self-directed nature of culture learning means that when someone starts to give you rules for what to do in one situation or another, you should be cautious with that advice. When someone starts to become a teacher, it short-circuits the process of culture learning and artificially levels all circumstances into a few general categories. Most of the time, the information is poor advice. The people who come from the community are experts, so you should be hesitant to accept cultural explanations from other expats.

Being a part of a community of learners who are observing and sharing their insights can be a powerful way to grow. Even more powerful is when you become part of the community of people from your new culture. When you gather with people who live in the area, you begin to form natural relationships that allow you to see firsthand how they respond in each situation. You can ask questions with confidence because you already have a relationship with those people. You can learn by observing and by asking within the safety of relationships that already exist.

Where do you find relationships like that? What communities are suited for this kind of learning? For Christian workers, the local church is a great starting place. Getting involved in a local congregation unites you with people from the unfamiliar culture whose beliefs you can relate to. This gives a head start on learning.

If you have a hobby, that can make for a good community. If you like sports, find a local league where you can participate. That community will help you learn a lot about life in that culture! If your reason for being in another culture has to do with your profession, then your professional relationships can be a community for learning. Schools, neighborhoods, local parks, adult education programs, or volunteer opportunities can all lead to community involvement and opportunities to learn the culture.

Again, this may require some attitude adjustment. There will definitely be times when you just don't want to go to the practice or class. Discouragement and learning fatigue are real parts of cultural adjustment. Having the attitudes of persistence, flexibility, and intentionality are all key to staying in community and learning new lifestyles. Being a part of a community that is either learning together or that is a context for learning becomes a keystone habit in its own right – it opens the door for many other habits.

ATTITUDES FOR SUCCESS

The point of this chapter has been to consider the attitudes of a culture learner. Just as there are key skills that help you to learn a new culture, there are also attitudes that will lead to growth and effective ministry. The process is a combination of outward skills and internal decisions, where you set the attitudes of your heart. It is important to choose what will encourage good culture learning and reject what will alienate you from the people you want to reach. Fight the good fight in your ministry by choosing to enter every situation with a positive attitude.

CHAPTER REVIEW

- What are the attitudes of a self-directed learner?
- What are the stages of intercultural sensitivity?
- How important is self-discipline in learning?

PUT IT INTO PRACTICE

- Review the DMIS. Honestly assess your mindset and identify what stage you are in. Do you need to improve your attitudes? How can you go about getting to the final stage?
- What attitudes do you feel you have most of the time? What attitudes do you need to improve?
- Do you think this is an exhaustive list of attitudes? Make a list of other attitudes that would be required for self-directed learning. How can you implement these attitudes?
- Withholding judgment is key when you are in a new culture. Think of some instances where you didn't withhold judgement, but you wish you had. Come up with a cue that you will think of when you are in an uncomfortable situation and you need to withhold judgment.

CHAPTER TEN

Tying it All Together

Sometimes the very best way to start an intercultural journey is to take a walk around your neighborhood. Then, walk a concentric circle a little wider than that first block. Finally, go out a third block and walk around again. Take that three-level walk at 9:00 in the morning on a business day, and then at 5:30 pm on another business day, and then at noon on a weekend. The hours and distances may vary, but you will start to see the multiple patterns of life that surround you right here and right now!

Your intercultural journey starts with a walk around the block. Where will it lead?

It might be that you are planning to head to another part of the world. You'll live as an expat among a group of people whose patterns of life are different from yours. The ideas shared in this book will help you to settle into life with that new community.

It might be that you are not the one traveling, but as you take your walk you start to see how many of your neighbors have traveled. They now live close to you but it is very possible that they come from all over the world.

Whether you are the one traveling or the one receiving people into your community, the tools introduced in this book are meant to help you learn the lifestyle of those neighbors. It turns out that the very tools that an intercultural worker needs for effective ministry in a different culture are also tools that can help a local church to engage with culturally diverse communities and neighborhoods. No one can really explain all the details of a culture but an intercultural worker can learn them little by little. In the same way, no one can teach you about those who have come from afar to your own neighborhood, but you can learn!

The following is a succinct review of how to learn what no one can teach you.

Chapter 1 set up the journey. You are aiming to bridge your heart and mind with the hearts and minds of those from an unfamiliar culture. This journey is more about relationships than physical location. If you keep this journey in mind through every action, you will have a consistent perspective and goal.

In chapter 2 you read about the goals that God is working toward. Every tribe, every language, every people group, and every nation will come to know him. Knowing that God is seeking and working toward that goal, the questions you can ask include, "How am I joining in that vision? What skills and attitudes am I building to put myself in touch with a new people group?"

The interpersonal side of intercultural work was the focus of chapter 3. It is definitely true that the patterns of life are different between people of different cultures. The focus is not rote, as if memorizing their holidays and table manners will build the intercultural bridge you need. Those facts and descriptions of acceptable manners might be important, but even more important is the ability to build bridges of relational interaction with people from that other group. Brain studies on syncing give great vocabulary for this goal of interpersonal relationships that lead to deepened understanding of both personal and cultural habits.

Chapter 4 focused on the goal of relationships with others. You must understand the importance of horizontal interpersonal relationships and vertical relationships between people and God. The amazing truth that God seeks to be in relationship with his creation is at the root of everything else in this book. God faithfully walks with you and asks you to love and serve well.

Chapter 5 moved into discovering the life patterns of a people group and figuring out how to learn those patterns. The core idea of this book is drawn from that discussion about learning and teaching. There are things that no one can teach you but that you can learn by directing yourself. This is especially the case in intercultural settings. No one could possibly put together all of the details that would fully and accurately describe the lifestyle of a specific group of people. Even if that kind of exhaustive resource existed, you could never absorb it all just by reading or listening. What you can do is know how to learn. You can learn to live and be effective in an unfamiliar culture.

Chapter 6 described the tool called The Culture Tree. Culture learning includes a lot of variations and pieces that all interact. The way people live at home, behave in the office, shop in the market, and worship are all parts of one whole. Culture learning is about the details and the big picture at the same time. That is one of the reasons why the tree metaphor works. There are many different internal elements to the tree and lots of details that you can study. Every small detail plays a vital role for the large tree. Culture is the life patterns, behaviors, and beliefs of a people group. It is unified and also divisible into many categories. The roots are different from the shoots, which are different from the fruits. The differences matter, but they still make up the holistic tree.

As you find new insights in the details, the large concepts, the patterns, and the values of a new culture, you can start to draw those elements into a graphic that looks like a tree. Seeing how the pieces of organization, history, and lessons all fit together with the other parts of The Culture Tree will give you a road map for effective life and work. It will be possible to sync with your neighbors because you are not stumbling over the details of organizational patterns or thought preferences. You will see how things are done in the unfamiliar social environment and you will enter into the patterns of the people.

In chapters 7 and 8 the focus was on the skills that will help you to learn the patterns of a people group. These tools will be necessary in order to assimilate into an unfamiliar culture.

- The Languages of Culture
- Asking questions
- Paying attention
- WTGA Learning Cycle
- Being intentional
- Sympathy and empathy
- Building bridges
- Involvement
- Taking notes
- Consulting experts
- Consuming media
- Building healthy habits

Chapter 9 continued building the toolbox for culture learning, but this time the focus was internal rather than external. If it's important to have objective tools like note-taking and The Languages of Culture, it is just as important to have the attitudes of a learner. In this chapter you learned about the stages of intercultural sensitivity – denial, defense, minimization, acceptance, adaptation, and integration. You also read about some needed attitudes for culture learning.

- Flexibility
- Withholding judgment
- Self-direction
- Forming habits

- Self-Discipline
- Community

As you come to the end of this book, here is a short summary of what you should know.

The patterns of life that a group shares are innate and impact every generation. It would be impossible to teach a culture to you, but you can still learn!

Learn by building relationships, knowing that as you walk with God he will open your eyes and your mind to understand the people he has sent you to. Things that seem totally baffling will all of a sudden make perfect sense when a friend from a new culture lives the pattern out before you.

Learn deliberately by being self-directed, active, and engaged in the process. Your own curiosity is one of the strongest tools for becoming effective in living and serving in an unfamiliar culture!

Learn deliberately by using the tools for culture learning, observing what is happening, asking for insight, and writing notes that will help you to see patterns.

Learn deliberately by cultivating a healthy attitude as a self-directed learner. Understand the ties that you have with people through common humanity, and have an attitude of respect and empathy. Your goal is not for them to become like you but for them to enter into a relationship with their creator. If you can keep that goal in front of you, the correct attitudes will follow!

May you develop a lifelong habit of growth in your understanding of the patterns of people around you. May that common understanding of life lead to many opportunities to talk about the author of life, the one whose truth is spreading until it reaches every tribe, language, people, and nation!

Endnotes

1. Worldometer. "Worldometer - Real Time World Statistics." Worldometer, 2021, www.worldometers.info.

2. "How Many Languages Are There in the World?" Ethnologue, 23 Feb. 2021, www.ethnologue.com/guides/how-many-languages.

3. Juan, Stephen. "What Are the Most Widely Practiced Religions of the World?" The Register, 7 Dec. 2018, www.theregister.com/2006/10/06/the_odd_body_religion.

4. Hasson, Uri. "This Is Your Brain on Communication." TED Talks, 10 May 2016, www.ted.com/talks/uri_hasson_this_is_your_brain_on_communication/up-next?language=en.

5. Smith, Donald. Creating Understanding. Zondervan, 1992.

6. Wan, Enoch, and Mark Hedinger. Relational Missionary Training: Theology, Theory & Practice. Urban Loft Publishers, 2017.

7. Balswick, Jack, et al. The Reciprocating Self: Human Development in Theological Perspective. IVP Academic, 2005.

8. Kim, Natalie. "Relational Intercultural Training Model for Practitioners of Business as Mission." March 2021. Western Seminary, EdD dissertation.

9. Dehaene, Stanislas. How We Learn: Why Brains Learn Better Than Any Machine . . . for Now. Penguin Books, 2021.

10. Hammond, Zaretta. Culturally Responsive Teaching and The Brain. Thousand Oaks, Canada, SAGE Publications, 2014.

11. Hedinger, Mark, et al. "The Culture Tree: A Powerful Tool for Mission Research and Training." Global Missiology, 24 July 2020, ojs.globalmissiology.org/index.php/english/article/view/2363.

12. Wohlleben, Peter, et al. The Hidden Life of Trees. David Suzuki Institute, 2016.

13. Doucleff, Michaeleen. "Rice Theory: Why Eastern Cultures Are More Cooperative." NPR, 8 May 2014, www.npr.org/sections/thesalt/2014/05/08/310477497/rice-theory-why-eastern-cultures-are-more-cooperative.

14. Dunbar, Robin. "Dunbar's Number." New Scientist, 2021, www.newscientist.com/definition/dunbars-number.

15. Hofstede, Geert, et al. Cultures and Organizations: Software of the Mind, Third Edition. 3rd ed., McGraw-Hill Education, 2010.

16. Trompenaars, Fons, and Charles Hampden-Turner. Riding the Waves of Culture: Understanding Diversity in Global Business. Nicholas Brealy Publishing, 2015.

17. Meyer, Erin. The Culture Map. PublicAffairs, 2014.

18. Hoffman, Edwin and Verdooren Arjan. Diversity Competence: Cultures Don't Meet People Do. Uitgeverij Coutinho, 2018.

19. Molinsky, Andy. Global Dexterity. Amsterdam, Netherlands, Reed Business Education, 2013.

20. Livermore, David A. Expand Your Borders: Discover Ten Cultural Clusters. Cultural Intelligence Center, 2013.

21. Nisbett, Richard. The Geography of Thought. Amsterdam, Netherlands, Amsterdam University Press, 2004.

22. Duhigg, Charles. The Power of Habit. New York, United States, Penguin Random House, 2014.

23. Bennett, Milton. "DMIS Model." IDRInstitute, 19 Apr. 2021, www.idrinstitute.org/dmis.

24. Middleton, Julia. "Cultural Intelligence: What Is Core and Flex?" YouTube, uploaded by Common Purpose Charitable Trust, 27 May 2014, www.youtube.com/watch?v=trPOurwfB4w.

25. Knowles, Malcolm. Self-Directed Learning. Cambridge Book Co, 1983.

26. Shaules, Joseph. The Intercultural Mind. Quercus, 2015.

27. "Hofstede Insights Organisational Culture Consulting." Hofstede Insights, 17 Nov. 2021, www.hofstede-insights.com.

About the Author

Mark Hedinger is the executive director of CultureBound, a non-profit ministry based in Portland, Oregon, United States. He holds a Doctorate of Intercultural Studies along with a Master of Divinity. Mark and his wife, Karen, spent 12 years living and teaching in Mexico. He has taught in a variety of international locations and serves in a multicultural church.

If you would like to contact Mark, you can email him at Mark.Hedinger@CultureBound.org, or submit a contact form on the CultureBound website at www.CultureBound.org.

Notes

151

Made in the USA
Columbia, SC
29 August 2022